Valentina's
4 SEASONS
COOKBOOK

Valentina's

4 SEASONS COOKBOOK

Valentina Harris

Food photography by Jean Cazals

CASSELL&CO

For Garry, the biker poet

I would like to thank Maggie Ramsay for patiently steering this book through the initial stages of its intricate journey. Surely, never has one book had so many versions! For the idea and making it all happen, my thanks go to Margaret Little; for her grace and calm in the midst of our final editorial storm, thank you to Eluned Jones; and last, but by no means least, many thanks to the design team David Rowley, Clive Hayball and Nigel Soper for making the book look so beautiful.

First published in the United Kingdom in 2000 by Cassell & Co

Text copyright © Valentina Harris 2000
Design and layout copyright © Cassell & Co 2000
Design Director David Rowley
Location shots © John Heseltine and Kim Sayer
Food photography by Jean Cazals

Distributed in the United States of America by Sterling Publishing Co., Inc.
387 Park Avenue South, New York, NY 10016-8810

A CIP catalogue record for this book is available from the British Library

ISBN 0 304 35388 4

Printed and bound in Italy

Cassell & Co
Wellington House
125 Strand
London WC2R 0BB

contents

introduction

One of the many things about Italian food that thrills me so much is how the cooking reflects, respects and understands the seasons of the year and the gifts that each season gives us. Acknowledging and embracing each of the seasons means that you can cook with anticipation! This is a really wonderful, exciting and fulfilling celebration. It is also humbling, and the humility of Italian food is one of the things that makes it so universally popular. We may well have developed so much and so far as a human race to be able to fly exotic and not so exotic ingredients thousands of miles across continents and oceans, but does the flavour of a super-refrigerated slice of marlin really taste better than the first, freshly caught mackerel of the season? Which tastes better and more stirringly: a strawberry from a far flung corner of the globe in January, or a sun-warmed strawberry from a local farm in the height of its rightful season?

The seasons of the year, and the produce they bring to our tables, have a pattern and a rhythm that is also part of the pattern and rhythm of cooking. For me, the two have always gone hand in hand. My earliest memories of vast meals being prepared at home is that there was always a certain degree of discussion about what was in season and what wasn't. That which was in season was considered fit for the table, that which was not was simply postponed. The first loquats (*nespole*) of the spring were something to get excited about after months of citrus fruits; the frosted cardoons of early winter days were considered truly special and were treated as such in their cooking; autumn mushrooms and game were eagerly anticipated and received; and all the glowing fruits of the summer were as much a part of the season as the deckchairs in the garden and the irritating mosquitoes.

The recent renaissance of organic produce means a return to food that has a great deal more flavour. In many cases it also means enjoying food in its natural season. This can only be a good thing. Farmers' markets are an excellent source of fresh, seasonal ingredients of all kinds. If you haven't yet discovered the farmers' markets in your area, then you should make every effort to find out where and when they are and rediscover the joy of seasonal produce as fresh as only local, organic produce can be.

Ingredients that are in tune with the seasons will give you much better results. I am a 'don't mess with it' kind of cook, the sort who, like most Italian cooks, simply chooses the best possible ingredients that are available at the time, and then does as little as possible to them. I am proud of this because, in this way, the ingredients are allowed to sing out and give of their best. Trust me on this. In this book, I've brought together a collection of recipes grouped by season. They are almost all quick and easy to prepare, so that even with a busy lifestyle you can still eat delicious food that is in rhythm with the season. This is, after all, the way most Italians eat.

Whether you are making a simple pasta dish or a more elaborate fish casserole, the basic rules are always the same: find the best ingredients that are affordable, in season, and look, smell and feel good. Either dish can be unpalatable or delicious, depending first and foremost upon the prime ingredients, and secondly upon what you do to them. If you start to cook the Italian way, all other styles of cooking will become more easy and enjoyable, because Italian cooking forces you to use your imagination, intuition and all those other intrinsic qualities that belong to the best kind of cook, the instinctive cook.

The one thing you cannot be taught is how to cook instinctively. Cookery courses can teach you about technique, can introduce you to ingredients you might previously not have considered, and can take you through the most daunting of recipes. But a real cook, a cook who is really outstanding, is a cook who uses their heart and their intuition in the kitchen. This is how most Italians cook, because they live to eat and their enjoyment of food and of cooking it with passion, flair and joy goes far beyond the necessity merely to keep body and soul together. If you want to cook Italian food that tastes like Italian food, then you need to follow some of the basic principles of the Italian kitchen. The simplest, most spartan of recipes can go completely wrong if not cooked with pride and care, and if the prime ingredients were not of the best possible quality and freshness when you started to prepare them. It is not really more difficult to cook a longer, more involved recipe, it is simply more time consuming.

It is my hope that you will enjoy all the recipes, anecdotes and essays in this book and that it will become a friend in the kitchen, as all our favourite cookery books do. I wish you happy meals around the table with your loved ones, and many hours of joy in the kitchen discovering these recipes and elaborating upon them as you wish in order that they may become as much yours as they are mine.

BUON APPETITO!

prima

vera spring

the pulse of spring The first ingredient that makes its way tentatively on to the scene to start the spring season in Italy is, for me at least, the tender and slightly sour loquat, which we call *nespole*. This is an oval, yellow fruit, about the size of a plum, with a thin skin and up to four shiny brown stones in its centre. It cannot be described as lovely to look at, and its uses in the kitchen are extremely limited, but to me the loquat always spelled the end of the winter and heralded the coming of all the other spring fruit and vegetables.

As the pulse of spring becomes stronger, the roadside sellers start to offer huge bunches of green, leafy globe artichokes for cooking in a myriad ways. In risotto and pasta, stuffed and baked, or dipped in batter and deep fried, the artichoke has always been a spring flavour, and I am glad the season is so long. The same cannot be said for asparagus, which is in season for a relatively short time in Italy. From the fattest, purple-tipped specimens to the thin, straggly-looking wild *spargit*, this vegetable also has a thousand and one uses in the kitchen. Personally, I like it best of all with freshly laid, buttery fried eggs and melting Fontina cheese.

At home, as the season progressed, there were suddenly lots more eggs available, as our hens busied themselves laying to celebrate their release from their long winter confinement. The kitchen would abound with fresh pasta that was as deeply golden and lustrous as the first sunny days, and cakes, biscuits, frittata and all manner of eggy recipes would be made in order to use them up.

As the days got warmer and the sea became calmer and clearer, with no more angry, cold waves churning up the sand and hurling trees off the shore and into the water, the fishing would start again. This meant rowing out to drop the nets in the chill of early morning, and returning to them in the afternoon to pull them safely ashore and sort out the catch while crouching on the sand.

No fish has ever tasted so fresh, clean and pure as the collection of oddments which we would carry home in a bucket of sea water suspended over the handlebars of our bicycles. The water would slop all over our legs as we pedalled deliberately over every bump in the road, just for the sheer hell of it. On arriving home, we would cook the fish as simply and speedily as possible for the very next meal. Sometimes we would simply leave the nets in the sea overnight, having dropped them at dusk, and be back on the beach in the morning filled with the thrill of anticipation of drawing them in again.

At this time of year, the most tender lamb is the meat of choice. The lamb is cooked so as to retain all its juicy succulence and is served alongside the best of the new season's vegetables, including peas, carrots, new potatoes and crisp cabbage.

With the first picnics and lunches taken outside to make the most of the precious sunshine, springtime in Italy means rediscovering the pleasure of eating food in the open air. The buzz of outdoor activity, the sense of a world waking up to the joys of the season after a long, dark, wet winter, and all the work that needs to be done to the vegetable garden, the vines, the olive groves, all this makes us feel part of the season and gives us a glimpse of the wonders of the long, hot summer just around the corner.

baked artichokes with parmesan and butter
carciofi al forno con parmigiano e burro

SERVES 2

2 large globe artichokes
½ lemon
1 garlic clove, finely chopped
2 tablespoons freshly chopped mint
3 tablespoons freshly grated
   Parmesan
sea salt and freshly milled
   black pepper
50 g (2 oz) unsalted butter

Snap off the artichokes' stems and pare away the outer skin until it is very pale green, almost whitish. Cut it into thin slices and sprinkle with lemon juice to prevent it from blackening.

Now rip off the artichokes' outer leaves until you are left with a central core of tender leaves, very pale coloured at the bottom and dark green at the tip. Cut off the hard tips and rub all over with the lemon. Open out the leaves enough to scrape away all the furry choke from the centre.

Mix together the sliced stems, garlic, mint, cheese and seasoning. Use this mixture to fill the cavity of both artichokes. Put the artichokes into a saucepan small enough for them to fit snugly. Put a knob of butter in the pan and push the remaining butter into the centre of the artichokes on top of the garlic and mint mixture. Pour in a little cold water, enough to come about 2 cm (1 inch) up the sides of the pan, cover tightly and place over a medium heat.

Depending upon how large or how fresh the artichokes are, it will take as little as 10–12 minutes or as much as half an hour until they are just tender all the way to the centre – test with a skewer or a long thin knife. Add a little more water if the artichokes need to cook further. You can serve them hot or cold and on their own, or with a plain grilled steak, chop or chicken breast.

This is one of my favourite ways of eating my favourite vegetable. It is well worth the fiddly preparation just to feel the flavours of mint, garlic and artichoke blend together in your mouth. Perfect.

eggs with asparagus and fontina
uova con asparagi e fontina

SERVES 2

2 tablespoons unsalted butter
200 g (7 oz) asparagus spears,
   cut into sections about 3 cm
   (1 inch) long
1 garlic clove, thinly sliced
100 g (3½ oz) fontina cheese,
   cubed
4 eggs, beaten
freshly milled black pepper
2 tablespoons freshly grated
   Parmesan
50 g (2 oz) thinly sliced Parma ham,
   cut into ribbons

Melt half the butter in a saucepan and fry the asparagus very gently. When it is tender but still brilliant green, add the garlic and the rest of the butter. Cook for a further 2 minutes, stirring gently.

Meanwhile, stir the cheese into the beaten eggs and season with black pepper. Add to the asparagus and stir very gently until thickened and scrambled. Transfer to warmed plates and sprinkle with the Parmesan. Arrange the Parma ham over the eggs and serve at once with plenty of crusty bread.

I remember eating this for the first time when we went to clear out some friends' country retreat at the end of a long cold winter. Shutters and windows were flung open so that the fresh air and quickly warming sun could chase away the winter blues. At lunchtime, we lit a camping gas stove outside and sat in the sunshine with our feast and plenty of rough red wine. It tasted especially good because we had picked the diminutive wild asparagus from the garden, but it is equally delicious even without picking your own.

asparagus and pea risotto
risotto d'asparagi e piselli

SERVES 6

500 g (1 lb) asparagus
sea salt and freshly milled
    black pepper
75 g (3 oz) unsalted butter
1 small leek, chopped
500 g (1 lb) risotto rice
500 g (1 lb) fresh peas, podded,
    or 250 g (9 oz) frozen petit pois
1.5 litres (2¾ pints) chicken or
    vegetable stock, kept just below
    boiling point
50 g (2 oz) Parmesan,
    freshly grated
1 tablespoon chopped fresh mint

Boil the asparagus with a large pinch of sea salt for about 6 minutes or until just tender. Drain, reserving the cooking liquid, and leave the asparagus to cool.

Melt half the butter in a large saucepan and fry the leek for about 5 minutes, until soft. Cut the asparagus into small pieces, leaving the heads intact. If the end of the stalk is very tough, scrape out the inside with a knife and discard the rest.

Add the rice to the leek and stir it around until it is heated through and shining. Then add the first ladleful of asparagus cooking liquid. Stir until the liquid has been absorbed, then add some more. Add the peas and stir through. Continue to add the liquid, making sure it is hot. Always add small amounts and wait for the rice to absorb the liquid before you add more. When you run out of the asparagus liquid, begin to add the stock. Continue adding liquid in this way for about 20 minutes, until the rice is cooked and swollen but still firm in the middle.

Stir in the Parmesan and mint and season to taste with pepper. Remove from the heat, cover and leave to stand for about 3 minutes. Serve at once, on warmed plates.

Tender, fresh green peas, bursting with sweetness, blend perfectly with the fresh twig, sappy flavour of asparagus. The leek is essential: onions or shallots are too strong for the delicacy of the vegetables.

spinach gnocchi with ricotta
malfatti di spinaci con ricotta

SERVES 4 TO 6

1.25 kg (2½ lb) spinach, washed
   and steamed
2 eggs, beaten
2 egg yolks
2 tablespoons single cream
250 g (9 oz) fresh ricotta,
   whisked with a fork to make it
   as light as possible
150 g (5 oz) Parmesan, grated
a large pinch of grated nutmeg
salt and freshly milled black pepper
3–6 tablespoons plain flour
100 g (3½ oz) unsalted butter,
   melted

Squeeze as much water as you can out of the spinach, using your hands. Chop it very finely (you could use a food processor) or rub it through a food mill.

Gradually and lightly mix in the eggs, egg yolks and cream. Mix the ricotta lightly into the spinach with half the Parmesan. Season to taste with nutmeg, salt and pepper.

Bring a large saucepan of salted water to the boil.

With a very light touch and using as little flour as possible, make the spinach mixture into small balls using your hands. Be miserly with the flour, or you will end up with rubbery gnocchi. When the water boils, drop them into the pan in very small batches. When they float up to the surface, after about 2 or 3 minutes, they are cooked. Using a slotted spoon, transfer them to a warmed serving dish. Drizzle with the melted butter and sprinkle with a little Parmesan. Repeat until all the spinach mixture has been used up. Serve at once.

These should be as light as a feather, pale green and shiny from the butter – and so delicious! Perfect for celebrating springtime.

spinach and ricotta tart
crostata salata di spinaci e ricotta

MAKES A 30 CM (12 INCH) TART

for the pastry:

350 g (13 oz) plain flour
180 g (6 oz) chilled unsalted butter,
cut into small pieces
a large pinch of dried sage
50 g (2 oz) Parmesan, finely grated
½ lemon
1 egg yolk

for the filling:

1 kg (2 lb) chard or spinach,
washed and picked over
500 g (1 lb) ricotta
3 egg yolks
75 g (3 oz) Parmesan, grated (with
a little extra for grating on top)
a large pinch of grated nutmeg
sea salt and freshly milled pepper

Put the flour and butter in a food processor and process until it resembles breadcrumbs. Alternatively, use your fingertips to lightly rub the butter into the flour. Add the sage and Parmesan, then the lemon juice, egg yolk and just enough cold water to bind the pastry together. Wrap and leave to rest in the refrigerator for 1 hour.

Preheat the oven to 180–190°C/350–375°F/gas mark 4–5. Grease and lightly flour a 30 cm (12 inch) tart tin.

For the filling, cook the spinach without additional water in a large saucepan. Drain and squeeze dry. Chop the spinach coarsely and mix with the ricotta, egg yolks, half the Parmesan, nutmeg, salt and pepper.

Roll out the pastry and line the tart tin. Fill with the spinach mixture and sprinkle with the remaining Parmesan. Bake until lightly browned and set. Serve hot or cold, as a first or main course.

A fantastically easy tart with a sophisticated flavour. If you are in a great hurry, you could use frozen pastry instead of making this lovely lemon and sage version.

spinach, parma ham and avocado salad
insalata di spinaci, prosciutto e avocado

SERVES 4

500 g (1 lb) fresh young spinach,
   well washed
8 slices Parma ham
1 large or 2 small avocados, neatly
   sliced or cubed and tossed in the
   juice of ½ lemon
1 garlic clove, crushed to a purée
2 tablespoons red wine vinegar
sea salt and freshly milled
   black pepper
4 tablespoons extra virgin olive oil
1 teaspoon mustard
ciabatta or other coarse Italian
   bread, warmed, to serve

Dry the spinach leaves carefully in a cloth or salad spinner and arrange in a salad bowl. Cut the ham into slivers with a pair of scissors and scatter over the spinach. Arrange the avocado around the edge of the spinach.

Mix the crushed garlic with the vinegar, salt and pepper. Gradually add the oil, stirring constantly, then mix in the mustard. Alternatively, put all the ingredients in a screw-top jar and shake the jar vigorously. Pour the dressing over the salad and serve with warm bread.

You can put this together very quickly using tender, new crop spinach. No cooking is required, but warming the bread improves the overall effect. Follow with a selection of cheeses, some fresh fruit or ice cream. Alternatively serve the salad as a second course after a light pasta dish.

pancakes with ricotta and sun-dried tomato paste
crespoline di ricotta e pomodori secchi

SERVES 2

for the batter:
125 g (4 oz) plain white flour
½ teaspoon salt
2 eggs, beaten
300 ml (10 fl oz) milk, or a mixture
   of milk and water
unsalted butter or sunflower oil
   for frying

for the filling:
250 g (9 oz) ricotta
3–4 tablespoons sun-dried
   tomato paste
about 10 fresh basil leaves, torn
   into small pieces
3–4 tablespoons freshly grated
   Parmesan
sea salt and freshly milled pepper

to garnish:
sprigs of basil and a few sun-dried
   tomatoes, sliced thinly

Preheat the oven to 190°C/375°F/gas mark 5.

To make the batter: whisk the flour, salt, eggs and milk together to make a smooth, fairly thin batter. Make sure there are no lumps whatsoever!

Heat a frying pan, then add a small lump of butter or about ½ teaspoon of sunflower oil. Pour in just enough batter to cover the bottom of the pan, swirling it around to cover the pan evenly. Cook for about 1 minute, then flip it over and cook the other side for another minute. Tip the cooked crespoline out on to a plate.

To make the filling: mash the ricotta until smooth and mix it with the sun-dried tomato paste, basil and half the Parmesan. Moisten with a little of the oil from the tomato paste and season to taste.

Oil an ovenproof dish. Divide the filling between the pancakes and roll them up. Place them in the oiled dish, brush with a little oil from the sun-dried tomato paste and sprinkle with the remaining Parmesan.

Place in the oven until heated through and golden brown on top, about 15 minutes. Serve at once, garnished with fresh basil leaves and a few strips of sun-dried tomatoes.

sheep's milk ricotta is at its most superb in the spring. The lambing ewes have excess milk which the farmers use to make Pecorino and ricotta. This amount of batter makes 12 pancakes; the filling is enough for 4 pancakes.

tagliatelle with an avocado sauce
tagliatelle con salsa di avocado

SERVES 4

2 ripe avocados, peeled and stoned

3 tablespoons mascarpone, ricotta
or crème fraîche

3 tablespoons freshly grated
Parmesan

sea salt and freshly milled
black pepper

3 tablespoons chopped fresh
flat-leaf parsley

400 g (14 oz) dried tagliatelle

Bring a large saucepan of salted water to a rolling boil.

Meanwhile, mash or process the avocados with the mascarpone, ricotta or crème fraîche. Stir in the Parmesan and season with plenty of pepper. Add a little of the boiling water to help blend the sauce, then stir in half the parsley. Adjust the seasoning, adding salt if necessary.

Cook the pasta in the boiling salted water until tender, then drain and return to the warm saucepan. Add the sauce and stir thoroughly to coat the pasta, then serve at once on warmed plates, sprinkled with the remaining parsley.

The pale green colour of the avocado always reminds me of the tender green of early spring.

fresh tagliatelle with cream, peas and pancetta
tagliatelle con panna, piselli e pancetta

SERVES 2

100 g (3½ oz) pancetta, cubed

1 tablespoon extra virgin olive oil

200 g (7 oz) best quality fresh
tagliatelle

1 tablespoon unsalted butter

150 ml (5 fl oz) cream (single,
whipping or double cream, or
crème fraîche)

150 g (5 oz) shelled fresh peas

sea salt and freshly milled
black pepper

3 tablespoons freshly grated
Parmesan

Bring a large saucepan of salted water to a rolling boil.

While the water is heating, fry the pancetta in the olive oil until
it is brown and mostly crisp.

Cook the pasta in the boiling water until al dente, then drain thoroughly
and return to the pan in which it was cooked. Add the butter and stir to
coat the pasta.

Meanwhile, warm the cream to just below boiling point, add to the
pasta and toss gently, then add the peas and pancetta, season with
black pepper and salt to taste and toss again. Serve at once on
warmed plates, sprinkled with the Parmesan.

Creamy, rich and indulgent, this is a really speedy pasta dish which
can be made with any pasta you like, but which works particularly
well with fresh tagliatelle. Tender young peas with their vibrant
green colouring are symbolic of springtime throughout Italy. At
other times of year this can be made with frozen petits pois.

pasta with caramelised red onions and ricotta
penne con cipolle dolci e ricotta

SERVES 4

4 tablespoons extra virgin olive oil

2 large red onions, finely sliced

sea salt and freshly milled black
   pepper

400 g (14 oz) dried penne

6 rashers smoked streaky bacon,
   grilled and chopped

5 tablespoons fresh ricotta

3 tablespoons freshly grated
   Parmesan

2 tablespoons chopped fresh
   flat-leaf parsley

Heat the oil and fry the onions very slowly, stirring frequently, until the onions are soft and sweet. Season with salt and pepper.

Bring a large saucepan of salted water to the boil. When the water boils, throw in the pasta and cook until tender. Drain thoroughly and return to the warm saucepan. Add the onions, bacon and ricotta and mix everything together thoroughly. Transfer to a warmed serving dish, sprinkle with the Parmesan and parsley and serve at once.

This makes the most of spring's freshest ricotta and the intensely sweet flavour of fat, juicy, purple onions.

pasta with a lemon and cream sauce
pasta al limone

SERVES 4

1½ tablespoons unsalted butter
grated zest of 2 large lemons
sea salt and freshly milled black
   pepper
400 g (14 oz) dried pasta
juice of 1 lemon
½ glass dry white wine
200 ml (7 fl oz) single cream
   or crème fraîche (half fat
   if preferred)
2–3 tablespoons finely chopped
   fresh flat-leaf parsley or basil
100 g (3½ oz) Parmesan, grated

Melt the butter in a large frying pan, add the lemon zest and fry gently for about 5 minutes.

Meanwhile, bring a large saucepan of salted water to a rolling boil. When the water boils, throw in the pasta and cook until tender.

While the pasta cooks, add the lemon juice to the butter and zest, then stir in the white wine and boil rapidly for about 2 minutes. Add the cream and black pepper to taste.

Drain the pasta thoroughly, then add to the cream mixture and stir well to coat the pasta completely. Add the parsley or basil and half the Parmesan and mix again. Serve at once on warmed plates, sprinkled with the remaining cheese.

This light and simple pasta dish makes the most of those lemons that have wintered over and are now, in the spring, bursting with flavour and intensity.

linguine with a creamy prawn sauce
linguine rosa

SERVES 4

1 small leek or shallot, very
  finely chopped
25 g (1 oz) unsalted butter
250 g (9 oz) small raw prawns
4 tablespoons dry white wine
400 g (14 oz) dried linguine
sea salt and freshly milled
  black pepper
250 ml (8 fl oz) single or
  double cream
2 tablespoons chopped fresh
  flat-leaf parsley

Bring a large saucepan of salted water to a rolling boil.

Meanwhile, fry the leek or shallot in half the butter for a few minutes, until soft. Add the prawns and cook for 4–5 minutes, then add the wine and boil off the alcohol for 2 minutes. Season to taste with salt and pepper and remove from the heat.

Cook the pasta in the boiling water until tender. Drain thoroughly and return to the warm saucepan. Pour the cream over the prawns and return to the heat. Stir and heat through for about 1 minute, then pour this sauce over the pasta. Toss together thoroughly, add the parsley and toss again. Transfer to a warmed serving bowl and serve at once.

The pink colour of this dish always reminds me of the peach and apricot blossom that are synonymous with Italy's springtime.

red mullet with white wine
triglie al vino bianco

SERVES 4

8 red mullet fillets

2 tablespoons plain flour

3 tablespoons extra virgin olive oil

2 garlic cloves, crushed

3 sage leaves, rubbed

1 glass dry white wine

sea salt and freshly milled
    black pepper

Toss the fish fillets in the flour, just enough to coat them lightly.

Heat the oil in a wide frying pan and add the garlic and sage. When the oil is hot, remove and discard the garlic and sage, lay the fish in the pan and cook gently for about 4 minutes; as it cooks, baste the fish with a little of the wine. Turn and cook the other side for another 4 minutes or so. Transfer the fish to a warmed plate and season with salt and pepper.

Add the remaining wine to the pan and turn up the heat. Bubble and stir for about 3 minutes, then pour over the fish. Serve at once, with fresh peas and tiny new potatoes.

If you can, buy large mullet which can be filleted easily, as this is a very bony fish. Smaller fish can be cooked whole; just scrape off the scales, rinse the inside and pat dry. Great flavour, lovely texture.

grilled tuna steak
tonno alla griglia

SERVES 2

juice of 1 lemon
6 tablespoons extra virgin olive oil
1 teaspoon dried oregano
sea salt and freshly milled
   black pepper
2 fresh tuna steaks

Mix the lemon juice, olive oil, oregano and salt and pepper together in a shallow dish. Lay the tuna steaks in the dish and leave in the refrigerator to marinate for anything between 1 and 12 hours.

Heat the grill pan until it sizzles when you brush it with a little olive oil. Cook the fish for about 5 minutes on each side, depending upon the thickness of the steaks. Serve hot.

lamb with olives
agnello con olive

SERVES 4

750 g (1¾ lb) very young tender
   lamb, boned and sliced thinly
3 tablespoons plain flour
6 tablespoons olive oil
sea salt
125 g (4 oz) black olives, stoned
   and coarsely chopped
a large pinch of dried marjoram
½ dried red chilli pepper, chopped
juice of 1 lemon

Coat the lamb lightly in the flour, then shake off the excess. Heat the oil in a wide frying pan, then fry the lamb until well browned. Season with salt and then scoop the sealed lamb out of the pan and drain on kitchen paper.

Arrange the meat in a flameproof casserole dish with the olives, marjoram and chilli. Pour over the lemon juice and cover. Place over a low heat and simmer very gently until the meat is tender, about 30 minutes. Serve hot with potatoes and a green vegetable.

spring in sicily is the start of the season for tuna, which have been negotiating the straits of Messina for thousands of years. The meaty flesh is made moist and juicy with this simple marinade, which makes for a delicious contrast of flavours.

Tender sweet spring lamb is perfect with the salty, slightly bitter flavour of olives. In my childhood, this dish used to be cooked outside in an earthenware pot stuck in the glowing embers of a fire.

roman roast lamb
abbacchio alla romana

SERVES 4

1 kg (2 lb) shoulder or leg of lamb,
   cut into 5 cm (2 inch) chunks
3 tablespoons olive oil
knob of butter
1 lamb's kidney, cubed
sea salt and freshly milled
   black pepper
2 glasses dry white wine or water
2 large anchovies preserved in salt,
   or 5 canned anchovy fillets in oil
2 small sprigs of rosemary
4 garlic cloves, peeled
4– 5 tablespoons red wine vinegar

Wipe the meat carefully to remove any bone shards. Set a wide, deep, heavy-bottomed frying pan over a low heat. Add the oil and butter and heat for 5 minutes. Seal the meat and kidney in the hot fat, browning them all over. Add 250 ml (8 fl oz) water, season generously with salt and pepper, then lower the heat. Cover and simmer for 45 minutes, basting occasionally with a little water or wine and turning the meat from time to time.

Meanwhile, rinse the salted anchovies or drain the canned ones thoroughly. Pound the rosemary leaves with the anchovies and garlic. Stir in the vinegar and pour this mixture over the meat. Stir thoroughly and simmer for about 5 minutes to burn off the sharpness of the vinegar before serving.

Probably the ultimate spring recipe, the original calls for the very tiniest young lamb or abbacchio, which means it is an unweaned animal. This has the most tender texture and deliciously sweet flavour imaginable.

roasted lamb cutlets
costolette d'agnello al forno

SERVES 4

1 kg (2 lb) lamb cutlets, trimmed
   and wiped
juice and grated zest of 1 lemon
½ glass (85 ml/3 fl oz) dry
   white wine
1 large sprig rosemary
4 cloves garlic, chopped
sea salt and freshly milled
   black pepper
extra virgin olive oil

Put the cutlets in a roasting tin with the lemon juice and zest, wine, rosemary and garlic. Mix everything around with your hands, rubbing the other ingredients into the meat with your fingers. Add salt and pepper and rub those into the meat also. Drizzle with olive oil and turn the meat in the oil to cover. Leave to stand for about 15 minutes while you preheat the oven to 200°C/400°F/gas mark 6.

Slide the roasting tin into the oven to roast for about 20 minutes, or until the lamb is well browned and cooked through; turn it once or twice during the cooking time. Serve piping hot, with roasted new potatoes and salad, or boiled new potatoes and baby carrots.

Here is a simple and aromatic way of roasting lamb cutlets; the tangy lemon cuts the natural fattiness of the lamb perfectly. You could put some new potatoes in the oven to roast at the same time.

lamb cutlets with prosciutto and mozzarella
costolette d'agnello alla bolognese

SERVES 6

12 lamb cutlets
3 tablespoons plain flour
2 eggs, beaten
5 tablespoons dry white
 breadcrumbs
6 tablespoons olive oil
 (not extra virgin)
sea salt and freshly
 milled black pepper
125 g (4 oz) Parma ham,
 in very thin slices
150 g (5 oz) mozzarella,
 cut into 12 slices

Preheat the oven to 220°C/425°F/gas mark 7.

Trim the cutlets carefully and flatten them as much as possible with a meat mallet. Dip them lightly in the flour, then in the beaten eggs, and finally in the breadcrumbs.

In a large frying pan, heat the oil until sizzling, then fry the lamb cutlets on both sides until golden brown and crisp. Remove from the pan, drain thoroughly on kitchen paper and season to taste.

Arrange the cutlets on a baking sheet, lay a slice of ham and a slice of mozzarella on each cutlet and bake in the oven for 5 minutes, or until the cheese begins to run. Serve at once, with new potatoes and lightly cooked spinach or a rocket salad.

In Italy, except for in Bologna and parts of the north, lamb cutlets are seldom used other than for roasting very simply. Generally, lamb and mutton are used in stews; veal is the preferred meat for quick and easy dishes. This is a marvellous, quite rare recipe for tender spring lamb cutlets.

Ricotta cream is based on a traditional recipe from Rome. It should be made about three hours before you want to eat it, but is very easy to throw together. Strawberries with mascarpone is a deliciously simple dessert, which needs to be made the night before for best results. In Italy, the strawberry season starts early, with some juicy berries ready by late April and early May if the weather has been kind.

ricotta cream
crema di ricotta

SERVES 4

400 g (14 oz) very fresh ricotta or
   cream cheese
50 g (2 oz) icing sugar, sifted
3 egg yolks
4 tablespoons chopped mixed
   candied fruit
2 tablespoons chopped walnuts
4 tablespoons dark rum
1 tablespoon Marsala wine
200 ml (7 fl oz) whipping cream,
   whipped until fairly stiff

If you are using cream cheese instead of ricotta, whip it first to give it a lighter texture. Mix together the ricotta or whipped cream cheese, icing sugar and egg yolks until you have a light, smooth mixture. Stir in the candied fruit, nuts, rum and Marsala. Carefully fold in the whipped cream.

Pour the mixture into individual bowls or stemmed glasses, put into the refrigerator and chill for 3 hours [or overnight]. Remove from the refrigerator just before serving.

strawberries with mascarpone
fragole al mascarpone

SERVES 2

1 punnet (about 250 g/9 oz)
   strawberries, hulled
3 tablespoons dry or medium-
   sweet white wine
1 tablespoon caster sugar
4 tablespoons mascarpone
2 tablespoons single cream
2 tablespoons soft brown sugar

Rinse the strawberries with the wine and cut them into even-sized pieces if necessary. Divide between two bowls or stemmed glasses and sprinkle with the caster sugar.

Mix the mascarpone and cream together until spreadable, then use to cover the strawberries completely. Sprinkle evenly with the brown sugar, place in the refrigerator and leave for several hours or overnight.

The brown sugar will run and marble the white cream, making it all look as good as it tastes.

soft ricotta cake with strawberries
torta morbida di ricotta con fragole

SERVES 6–8

300 g (11 oz) very fresh ricotta
   or cream cheese
300 g (11 oz) caster sugar
3 egg yolks, beaten with
   4 tablespoons milk
75 g (3 oz) plain flour, sifted twice
3 level teaspoons baking powder
grated rind of 1 large lemon
3 egg whites, chilled

to serve:
400 g (14 oz) fresh strawberries,
   washed, dried, hulled, and
   sliced if large
5 tablespoons Marsala wine
3 tablespoons caster sugar
4 tablespoons icing sugar

Preheat the oven to 160°C/325°F/gas mark 3. Butter a 30cm/12 inch cake tin very generously.

Whisk the ricotta or whipped cream cheese lightly with a balloon whisk, gradually adding the sugar, until the mixture is fluffy. Continue to whisk, blending in the egg yolks and milk, then the flour, baking powder and lemon rind.

Whisk the chilled egg whites until stiff peaks form, then gently fold them into the ricotta mixture. Pour the mixture into the cake tin and smooth it out with the back of a spoon. Bake for 45 minutes to 1 hour or until a thin metal skewer pushed into the centre of the cake comes out perfectly clean. Do not worry if the middle of the cake sinks a little, this is quite normal. Remove from the tin and leave on a wire rack to cool completely.

Lightly mix the strawberries with the Marsala and sugar and leave to marinate for 30 minutes.

Serve the cake with the strawberries; sift the icing sugar over the cake just before serving.

springtime is traditionally when ricotta is at its freshest and best, and served with the first strawberries of the season this soft cake makes a marvellously easy dessert for any dinner or lunch party.

est

ate summer

summer bounty

The taste of summer in Italy for me is the unmistakable, sweet flavour of freshly picked, sun-warmed tomatoes. In the vegetable garden at home the tomato canes reigned supreme and were covered in tomatoes of every hue of pale green, orange, yellow and red from June onwards.

To pick tomatoes that are warm from the sun, tomatoes that only need a quick rinse under a tap before being sliced and served with a drizzle of extra virgin olive oil, a light sprinkling of sea salt and perhaps a few torn-up leaves of basil, is really to eat food fit for the gods. At the end of summer, the ritual of stripping off the last, over-ripened fruits and turning them into oceans of tomato sauce for bottling was a magical time too, and the sauce lasted well into miserable February to remind us of those heady days even when the ice was sharp and hard on the ground.

All Mediterranean countries have a sensible custom of not spending hours slaving over a hot stove in the heat of the day, so often the bulk of heat-inducing cookery is done in the cool of the early morning. At home, anything that involved using the oven for long periods of time would be done good and early. At lunchtime, pasta, salads and other light dishes would be on the menu, and in the evening we almost always ate outside, with plenty of mosquito repellent on our skin and citronella candles burning. We'd light the barbecue and burn fragrant wood to grill meat or fish, and serve great dishes of potatoes roasted with garlic and rosemary and sliced lemons. Afterwards, there would be the delights of ice cream with soft fruits, gigantic peaches sliced into glasses of red wine, raspberries bobbing up and down in glasses of prosecco, or ice-cold slices of anguria (watermelon).

The local saying about anguria is 'la mangi, la bevi, e ti ci lavi la faccia' (you eat it, you drink it, and then you wash your face with it).

Later, we'd either go down to the beach to swim in the moonlight, play endless games of sardines or hide and seek in the pitch-dark garden, or ride our bikes down to the local bar and eat more ice cream.

One of the best things about food in the summer were the huge beach picnics that my mother organised for the household, often for twenty of us or more. At about noon, the busy, humming-with-seaside-activity beach would clear, with people going home for a long lunch and lazy siesta in the cool shade of a pine tree. Almost empty, the beach would take on the appearance and the temperature of a great desert, with the heat rising visibly into the air.

Under our tendone (like a square beach umbrella with poles on each corner), we would gather to eat the picnic our housekeeper had brought us. The sand was hot enough to cook eggs in, and she'd always bring a few raw eggs so that we, as children, could experiment with how long it took to solidify them in their shells once they were buried. She would also bring us warm frittata with a myriad of vegetables in the mixture; flattened strips of chicken breast coated in breadcrumbs and quickly fried in oil; ripe, firm tomatoes and plenty of other wonderful things. Those picnics seem like food from another planet compared with the gritty sandwiches I have since consumed on far too many windswept British beaches!

The summers seemed like an endless feast of marvellous delights, and our appetites were always so sharp and keen, despite the heat. Those summer months represented the very best of the riches of our vegetable garden and only now do I truly appreciate how valuable those meals were.

courgette soup
minestra di zucchine

SERVES 4

1 tablespoon butter or vegetable oil
1 onion, finely sliced
1 carrot, finely chopped
1 stick of celery, chopped
1 garlic clove, crushed
6 courgettes, 5 roughly chopped
   and 1 grated
1.5 litres (2½ pints) vegetable stock
   or water
sea salt and freshly milled
   black pepper
1 tablespoon chopped fresh mint
a little double cream and a few
   sprigs of mint, to serve (optional)

Heat the butter or oil in a large saucepan. Add the onion, carrot, celery and garlic, cover and cook over a low heat for about 5 minutes. Add the chopped courgettes, stir through the onion mixture, cover and cook for another 5 minutes.

Add the stock or water and simmer for about 10 minutes, until all the vegetables are soft. Season to taste. Purée in a blender or food processor, then stir in the grated courgette and the mint. Serve at once, with a swirl or cream and a sprig of mint if desired.

Courgettes are the one vegetable that I always manage to grow successfully, so much so that I have now ventured into growing different varieties! One of the things I have discovered is that if the summer weather is inclement, it gives a better crop of courgette flowers, which can be coated in a light batter and deep fried; in some recipes they are first stuffed with a mixture of breadcrumbs or ricotta, herbs and Parmesan.

parsley salad
insalata di prezzemolo

SERVES 8

24 large juicy black olives, stoned

8 anchovy fillets, washed and dried

2 tablespoons salted capers,
   washed and dried

1 hard-boiled egg, shelled

5 large spring onions, very
   finely chopped

8 tablespoons extra virgin olive oil

2 tablespoons white wine vinegar

$\frac{1}{2}$ teaspoon best quality
   balsamic vinegar

freshly milled black pepper

a very large bunch of fresh parsley,
   about 500 g (1 lb), washed
   and dried

Chop the olives, anchovies, capers and hard-boiled egg finely. Put them all into a serving bowl together with the spring onions. Pour in the olive oil, vinegar and plenty of black pepper. Mix thoroughly and leave to steep for 15-30 minutes.

Take the leaves off the bunch of parsley and add to the other ingredients just before serving. Toss together quickly and serve with crusty bread.

My dear friend Henrietta Green, the highly acclaimed food writer and champion of British food, suggested that I include a parsley salad in this book, so here is my adaptation of her recipe. This unusual salad is a perfect first course as it is incredibly refreshing and sets the tastebuds alight.

prawn and olive salad
insalata di gamberoni con olive

SERVES 4

20 large, uncooked prawns in
    their shells
1 teaspoon salt
1 teaspoon red wine vinegar
8 firm, sweet plum tomatoes
2 tablespoons very finely chopped
    red onion
6 sticks of celery, trimmed and
    finely chopped
12 black olives, stoned and
    coarsely chopped
4 tablespoons coarsely chopped
    fresh flat-leaf parsley
4 teaspoons lemon juice
8 tablespoons extra virgin olive oil
sea salt and freshly milled
    black pepper

Wash the prawns in cold water. Meanwhile, bring a saucepan of water to the boil with the salt and vinegar. When the water boils, throw in the prawns and cook for 1 minute, then drain immediately and set aside to cool.

Drop the tomatoes into a bowl of boiling water for 1 minute to loosen the skins, then drain, peel and discard the seeds. Cut the tomatoes into small pieces.

As soon as you can handle the prawns without burning your fingers, shell and de-vein and put them into a serving bowl.

Add the onion and celery and mix together, then add the chopped tomatoes, olives, parsley, lemon juice and olive oil. Mix together, season to taste and serve. Do not dress the salad too soon, because the salt will draw juice out of the tomatoes and the result will be sloppy.

If large uncooked prawns prove hard to find you can make the salad with small, cooked prawns, although it won't be nearly as tasty. A must for summer parties al fresco.

valentina's caesar salad
insalata valentina (alla "caesar salad")

SERVES 4 AS A FIRST COURSE, 2 AS A MAIN COURSE

1 large Cos lettuce or 2 hearts
   of romaine lettuce, washed
   and dried
3 tablespoons mayonnaise
3 tablespoons crème fraîche
2 tablespoons extra virgin olive oil
1 teaspoon anchovy essence
½ teaspoon white wine vinegar
sea salt and freshly milled
   black pepper
2 tablespoons milk
6 anchovy fillets, washed and dried,
   then chopped
4 tablespoons sunflower or olive oil
5 slices white bread, crusts
   removed, cut into cubes
1 tablespoon grated Parmesan
125 g (4 oz) pancetta, cubed
30 g (1 oz) Parmesan, shaved

Take the outer leaves of the lettuce and arrange them around the outside of a wide flat bowl. Cut the remaining leaves into bite-sized pieces and arrange them in a pile in the middle.

Mix together the mayonnaise, crème fraîche, olive oil, anchovy essence, vinegar and seasoning to taste. Slacken the dressing with milk until it reaches a thick pouring consistency; set it to one side until needed.

Sprinkle the anchovy pieces over the lettuce.

Heat the sunflower oil in a frying pan and fry the bread cubes until crisp and golden, turning frequently so that they don't burn. Turn the croûtons out on to absorbent kitchen paper and drain well. Sprinkle the grated Parmesan over them and toss to coat thoroughly. Scatter them over the lettuce.

Meanwhile, fry the pancetta in a hot pan until browned and crisp, then tip the pancetta and its fat over the salad. Pour the dressing over the salad and finish by sprinkling on the Parmesan shavings. Serve immediately with crusty bread.

This salad was created in the 1920s on July 4th in Tijuana, Mexico, by the Italian chef Caesar Cardini, using the few things he had left in the kitchen at the time; the original dressing is made with a raw egg. It appeals to me because it is an 'off the top of one's head' creation. This is my version.

pecorino salad
insalata di pecorino

SERVES 2

25 g (1 oz) unsalted butter,
  softened
8 slices of bread from a small
  Italian loaf, such as a sfilatino
1 large garlic clove, peeled
100 g (3½ oz) pancetta or smoked
  bacon, cubed
1 small head curly endive, washed
  and dried
50 g (2 oz) firm Pecorino, cubed
1 heaped tablespoon chopped
  fresh flat-leaf parsley

dressing:
a pinch of fine sea salt
freshly milled black pepper
1 teaspoon white wine vinegar
2 teaspoons lemon juice
4 teaspoons extra virgin olive oil
3 teaspoons sunflower oil

Preheat the oven to 150°C/300°F/ gas mark 2. Make the dressing, mixing all the ingredients together in the order given and whisking with a fork or a small balloon whisk until the oil is emulsified and the dressing is smooth.

Spread the butter on both sides of each slice of bread. Heat a frying pan and fry the bread on both sides until crisp and golden. Rub the fried bread with the peeled garlic and then place in the warm oven on a heatproof plate. In the same frying pan, quickly fry the pancetta until browned and crisp.

Cut the largest endive leaves into two or three pieces, place in a serving bowl and toss with the dressing. Crumble the cheese with a fork and add it and the bread to the salad. Toss together thoroughly. Scatter over the pancetta and the parsley, then serve immediately.

Make sure the cheese is mature enough to crumble without too much trouble, but don't buy cheese that is so hard and strong-tasting that it overpowers the other ingredients. By summer, Pecorino made in the spring is just about right.

italian warm potato salad
insalata di patate

SERVES 4–6

500 g (1 lb) new potatoes, washed
2 large handfuls of fresh basil
½ red onion, finely chopped
150 g (5 oz) ready-prepared organic
   salad leaves
300 g (11 oz) organic cherry
   tomatoes, halved
25 g (1 oz) Parmesan, grated

for the dressing:
5 tablespoons extra virgin olive oil
2 tablespoons good quality
   balsamic vinegar
1 garlic clove, very finely chopped
sea salt and freshly milled
   black pepper

Cook the potatoes in boiling lightly salted water until tender, approximately 15–20 minutes. Tear most of the basil into shreds, reserving some sprigs for garnishing. Drain the potatoes and cut in half while still hot. Combine the potatoes, onion and basil in a large bowl.

Put all the dressing ingredients into a screw-top jar and shake together until well blended and emulsified. You could do this in a blender if you prefer. Taste and adjust the seasoning. Pour the dressing over the warm potatoes and toss to coat all the ingredients.

To serve, arrange the salad leaves and tomatoes on a platter and spoon the warm potato salad on top. Sprinkle with the Parmesan and garnish with the basil leaves. Serve at once.

Potato salad, even in the middle of the summer, is always much nicer when it isn't icy cold. Dress the potatoes while they are still hot: they will absorb all the flavours from the basil and onions and the dressing. Use small, sweet new potatoes for the best results, and make sure they are cooked all the way through. For a different flavour, substitute rocket leaves for the basil. Add a few sun-dried tomatoes, cut into thin strips, for extra texture and sweetness.

green bean and chicken salad
insalata di pollo e fagiolini

SERVES 2

1 little gem lettuce, leaves
   separated
¼ oak leaf lettuce
½ head radicchio,
125 g (4 oz) fine green beans,
   topped and tailed
3 tablespoons olive oil
1 garlic clove, crushed
2 small chicken breasts, cut into
   finger-sized strips
sea salt and freshly milled
   black pepper

for the dressing:
2 tablespoons white wine vinegar
¼ teaspoon salt
½ teaspoon mustard
6 twists of freshly milled
   black pepper
8 tablespoons extra virgin olive oil

Wash and dry all the salad leaves thoroughly, tear the oak leaf lettuce and radicchio into bite-sized pieces, then arrange them in a wide salad bowl. Bring a saucepan of salted water to the boil and cook the beans until just tender.

Meanwhile, heat the olive oil in a small frying pan with the garlic, then quickly stir-fry the chicken strips until crisp and cooked through.

Put all the dressing ingredients into a screw-top jar and shake together until well mixed and thickened.

Drain the beans and tip them on to the salad leaves. Scatter the hot chicken over the beans and salad leaves, sprinkle with the dressing and serve at once.

This is a very quick summer dish that always manages to impress. The most important thing is to serve it before the salad leaves begin to wilt. For an even quicker result, buy tasty ready-cooked chicken, and then you will only need to cook the beans.

spaghetti with celery and blue cheese sauce
spaghetti al sedano e gorgonzola

SERVES 4

4 sticks of tender celery,
   finely chopped
50 g (2 oz) unsalted butter
sea salt and freshly milled
   black pepper
3 tablespoons double cream
200 ml (7 fl oz) milk
200 g (7 oz) blue cheese, cubed
400 g (14 oz) spaghetti
a few celery leaves to garnish

Bring a large saucepan of salted water to a rolling boil.

Meanwhile, fry the celery in the butter until very tender. Season and add the cream. Mix together, then remove from the heat and set aside.

Put the milk and blue cheese into another small saucepan and place over a low heat, stirring until the cheese has melted into the milk.

Cook the pasta in the boiling water until tender, then drain and return to the saucepan in which it was cooked. Pour in the blue cheese mixture and the cooked celery in its creamy sauce. Stir everything together and serve at once on warmed plates, garnished with the celery leaves.

I have put the perfect combination of blue cheese and celery together to create a marvellously simple pasta sauce. Blue cheese is great as a summer flavour, tangy and salty, it is delicious with all kinds of fruits, vegetables and salads.

creamy pesto pasta
pasta al pesto cremosa

SERVES 2

250 g (9 oz) linguine

100 g (3½ oz) peeled potato cubes, rinsed and dried, cooked until tender

100 g (3½ oz) fine green beans, topped and tailed, cooked until crisp

125 ml (4 fl oz) double cream

2–3 heaped teaspoons best quality pesto

sea salt and freshly milled black pepper

2 tablespoons freshly grated Parmesan

a few sprigs of basil, to garnish

Bring a large saucepan of salted water to the boil. Add the pasta and cook until tender. About 3 minutes before it is cooked, add the potatoes and beans to heat through with the pasta. Drain and return to the warm saucepan.

Add the cream and pesto and mix everything together thoroughly. Taste and adjust the seasoning. Serve at once on warmed plates; sprinkle with grated Parmesan and add a sprig or two of basil.

Opening a jar of good-quality Ligurian pesto, such as the renowned brand Sacla, opens up all sorts of possibilities, and even in the depth of winter it brings the flavour of an Italian summer into the kitchen. Here is my interpretation of the classic Ligurian style of serving pesto with pasta.

When I was a wild and wilful teenager growing up in Tuscany, during the long hot summers we never bothered to get up much before noon, as each night was spent partying until the early hours. Before going back to bed, we would all insist on eating something substantial. If dawn was breaking and we were at the beach, we would find the nearest bakery and buy baskets filled with bomboloni, the ultimate Tuscan doughnut, and then we'd fall in between the sheets, encrusted with sand and coarse granulated sugar. If it was still dark, Pasta ajo e ojo was our final snack. Here is that recipe, slightly smartened up by using black pasta, tinted with squid ink.

black tagliolini with olive oil and garlic

tagliolini neri ajo e ojo

SERVES 2

200 g (7 oz) black tagliolini
4 tablespoons extra virgin olive oil
2 garlic cloves, lightly crushed
2 teaspoons chopped fresh parsley
sea salt

Bring a large saucepan of salted water to a rolling boil, toss in the tagliolini, stir and boil for about 2 minutes, then drain thoroughly.

Meanwhile, heat the olive oil with the garlic until the garlic turns golden brown, then discard. Pour the hot flavoured oil over the tagliolini and toss together thoroughly. Sprinkle with the parsley and salt and serve immediately. If it is very late at night, retire after eating!

tagliatelle with courgettes, prosciutto,and balsamic vinegar

tagliatelle con zucchine e prosciutto condito
con aceto balsamico

SERVES 4

400 g (14 oz) tagliatelle
2 tablespoons olive oil
1 small red onion, thinly sliced
1 garlic clove, thinly sliced
2 courgettes, thinly sliced
4 tablespoons white wine
sea salt and freshly milled
    black pepper
4 slices of Parma ham,
    finely chopped
3 tablespoons ricotta cheese
4 tablespoons freshly grated
    Parmesan
3 teaspoons balsamic vinegar

Bring a large saucepan of salted water to the boil.

Meanwhile, heat the olive oil and fry the onion and garlic for about 4 minutes, then add the courgettes and fry for another 10 minutes. Add the wine, boil off the alcohol, then cover and simmer until the vegetables are soft. Then add the Parma ham and season to taste.

Toss the pasta into the boiling water and boil until tender. Drain well and return to the saucepan. Add the courgette mixture, ricotta and Parmesan. Toss over a high heat for a minute or two, then sprinkle with the balsamic vinegar, transfer to a warmed platter and serve at once.

pasta, grilled vegetables and pesto
pasta, verdure grigliate con pesto

SERVES 4, GENEROUSLY

1 aubergine, sliced lengthways,
   sprinkled with salt and left in a
   colander for 1 hour, then rinsed
   and dried
2 courgettes, thinly sliced
   lengthways
2 peppers, sliced lengthways
   and deseeded
1 large onion, peeled and sliced
   right across the centre into 8 flat,
   thick slices
4 tomatoes, sliced very thickly
100 ml (4 fl oz) olive oil, plus extra
   for serving
2 tablespoons chopped fresh
   flat-leaf parsley
sea salt and freshly milled
   black pepper
400 g (14 oz) dried fusilli or penne
3 tablespoons best-quality pesto

Bring a large saucepan of salted water to the boil.

Unless you are using a barbecue, heat the grill to medium. Grill each vegetable until just tender, brushing with olive oil. As soon as the vegetables are cooked, transfer them to a wide, shallow dish and sprinkle with chopped parsley, then season with salt and pepper. When all the grilled vegetables are in the bowl, sprinkle with the remaining olive oil. Keep the vegetables as warm as possible.

Add the pasta to the boiling water and cook until tender. Drain and return to the saucepan in which it was cooked. Add the vegetables to the pasta. Add the pesto and more salt and pepper to taste. Toss together thoroughly, adding more oil if necessary. Transfer to a warmed serving dish and serve at once.

When you see this recipe arranged on a dish, it just says: SUMMER! I like to grill my vegetables on the barbecue and cook the pasta on the stove, then combine the two elements and eat it while the vegetables' space on the barbecue is taken up by the meat for the second course.

fresh vegetable lasagne
lasagne magre

SERVES 6

1 onion, sliced

5 tablespoons olive oil

2 carrots, cubed

2 courgettes, cubed

125 g (4 oz) shelled peas

1 litre (1¾ pints) béchamel sauce
   (ready-made if you like)

500 g (1 lb) dried lasagne

125 g (4 oz) mushrooms, sliced

200 g (7 oz) Parmesan, grated

125 g (4 oz) tomatoes, peeled
   and chopped

150 g (5 oz) mozzarella, cubed
   or sliced

Preheat the oven to 200°C/400°F/gas mark 6.

Fry the onion in the olive oil until soft. Add the carrots, courgettes and peas and cook slowly for 10 minutes, uncovered.

Pour a layer of béchamel sauce into an oiled ovenproof dish (30 x 30 cm/ 12 x 12 inches) and cover with a layer of pasta. Add the first layer of vegetables, then a handful of sliced mushrooms, 2 tablespoons of Parmesan, and a handful of chopped tomatoes. Repeat until all the ingredients are used up, then add a layer of mozzarella on top of the last layer of béchamel. Place in the oven for 25 minutes. Leave to stand for 10 minutes before serving.

pasta with mascarpone, orange and basil
pasta al mascarpone, arancio e basilico

SERVES 4

400 g (14 oz) dried pasta

5 tablespoons mascarpone

grated zest of 1 orange

a handful of fresh basil leaves,
   torn into small pieces

3 tablespoons freshly grated
   Parmesan

sea salt and freshly milled
   black pepper

Bring a large saucepan of salted water to a rolling boil and add the pasta.

Mix the mascarpone with the orange zest, basil and Parmesan. Season with salt and pepper. Add enough hot water (3–4 tablespoons) from the pasta to loosen the sauce to the desired consistency.

When the pasta is tender, drain well, then return to the saucepan. Add the sauce and mix thoroughly. Serve at once on warmed plates, garnished with a sprig of fresh basil.

warm seafood salad
insalata di mare tiepida

SERVES 4

20 fresh mussels, scrubbed
and cleaned

40 fresh baby clams (vongole),
scrubbed and cleaned

1 bay leaf

1 lemon

200 g (7 oz) fresh squid, cleaned
and cut into strips and rings

180 g (6 oz) fresh small prawns

4 large fresh Mediterranean prawns

6 tablespoons extra virgin olive oil

3 tablespoons chopped fresh
flat-leaf parsley

sea salt and freshly milled
black pepper

salad leaves and lemon slices,
to serve

Leave the mussels and clams in a bucket of cold water overnight with the bay leaf and half the lemon.

Boil the squid in salted water for 25–30 minutes, until tender; set aside. Wash the prawns, then place in a small saucepan, cover with cold water, bring to the boil and cook for 1 minute. Drain and leave until almost cool before shelling.

When it is almost time to eat, steam the mussels and clams for about 8 minutes, discarding any that don't open. Remove the mussels and clams from their shells and put them in a warmed serving bowl with the prawns and squid. Mix them all together. Squeeze the juice from the reserved lemon half and add it to the seafood with the olive oil, parsley and pepper to taste. Add salt after mixing. Serve tepid, piled on to the salad leaves and garnished with lemon slices.

Seafood is deliciously light for the summer, but do be careful to eat only the freshest possible specimens. The overnight soaking helps to get the shellfish really clean.

grilled squid with red onion marmalade

seppie alla griglia con marmellata di cipolle rosse

SERVES 2

2 large red onions, finely sliced
2–3 tablespoons olive oil
2 tablespoons balsamic vinegar
sea salt and freshly milled
    black pepper
4 squid, cleaned
purple basil and flat-leaf parsley,
    to garnish

Fry the onions very slowly in a little olive oil until soft and caramelized; this will take around 20 minutes. Sprinkle with the balsamic vinegar and a little salt and pepper. Keep them over a very low heat, stirring frequently, until required; do not allow them to burn.

Meanwhile, slit the sides of the squid bodies and open them out flat, then lightly score both sides with a sharp knife in a criss-cross pattern to prevent them from curling up. Heat a griddle pan until searing hot. Brush the pan with olive oil, then grill the squid for about 1 minute on each side.

Spread the onion mixture between the 4 squid and remove from the griddle pan, allowing the squid to roll up slightly around the filling. Serve on warmed plates, garnished with a sprig of purple basil, a sprig of flat-leaf parsley and a little dollop of the onion marmalade.

Don't make the mistake of letting the marmalade get too sweet. If it tastes sickly in any way, add a drop or two of lemon juice to liven it up and give it a sharp note. The squid must smell and taste really fresh and should be buttery in texture.

71

swordfish steaks with tomato
pesce spada al pomodoro

SERVES 2

2 swordfish steaks
juice of ½ lemon
4 tablespoons olive oil
large pinch of dried oregano
sea salt and freshly milled
   black pepper
4 fresh, ripe, firm plum tomatoes
2 tablespoons extra virgin olive oil
6 black olives, stoned and chopped
½ avocado, peeled and cubed
1 tablespoons chopped mixed
   fresh herbs or fresh basil

Wash the fish, pat dry and lay it in a shallow bowl. In a separate bowl, mix the lemon juice, olive oil, oregano, salt and pepper. Pour this over the fish and massage well into the flesh. Leave in the refrigerator for about 2 hours, or overnight.

Drop the tomatoes into a saucepan of boiling water for 30 seconds, then scoop out and peel, discard the seeds and chop the tomato flesh into neat dice. Put the chopped tomato in a bowl with the olive oil, olives, avocado, herbs and salt and pepper to taste.

Heat the grill to medium. Brush the fish with the marinade and grill for about 4 minutes, then turn over, brush again with the marinade and cook for a further 2 minutes. Transfer to a warmed serving dish, spoon over the tomato mixture and serve at once.

swordfish, shark or tuna fish steaks can all be used for this recipe. These fish share the tendency to be very dry, so the marinating — allow 2 hours or overnight — is essential to create a moist, juicy texture. The fresh tomato sauce gives the fish a real lift, adding bite, juice and sweetness. The marinated fish is an obvious candidate for the barbecue, but whatever you do, don't overcook it.

sea bass baked in a salt crust
branzino al sale

SERVES 4

1 perfectly fresh sea bass weighing
   about 1.5 kg (3 lb)
about 1.5 kg (3 lb) sea salt
2 egg whites, beaten until foaming
   and thick

Preheat the oven to 200°C/400°F/gas mark 6. Clean and gut the fish, wash it thoroughly and pat dry. Protect the slit in the belly and the area around the gills with small pieces of foil tucked inside the fish. Mix the salt and egg whites together; this creates a really efficient crust, much better than salt on its own.

Choose an ovenproof dish large enough for the fish to fit comfortably both lengthways and widthways and allowing space for the salt packing. Line the dish with about half the salt mixture. Lay the fish on top, then cover completely with more salt. Pat it gently into place, making sure it is evenly spread and compact. Bake until the surface of the salt crust is beginning to look dark brown in places; this should take about 40 minutes.

Take the dish out of the oven and crack the salt crust with a large knife. Carefully remove the fish in portions, without the skin, and brush off any excess salt with a soft brush before serving. Offer a small jug of your best extra virgin olive oil for people to drizzle over their individual portions of this amazing fish.

This is one of those wonderful dishes that is simple to cook and never fails to impress. And before you ask, no, the fish does not taste incredibly or inedibly salty as a result of being cooked in this way.

cod fillets in anchovy butter
filetti di merluzzo al burro d'acciughe

SERVES 6

6 x 150 g (5 oz) fresh cod fillets
  or steaks
3 tablespoons plain white flour
2 eggs, beaten
4 tablespoons dried white
  breadcrumbs
8 tablespoons light olive oil or
  sunflower oil
6 salted anchovies, boned, rinsed,
  dried and chopped
100 g (3½ oz) unsalted butter
1 tablespoon white wine vinegar
3 tablespoons chopped fresh
  flat-leaf parsley

Dip the fish in the flour, then in the egg, then in the breadcrumbs. Heat the oil in a large frying pan until sizzling hot, then fry the fish for 3–5 minutes on each side, or until crisp and golden. Drain on kitchen paper and keep warm.

Put the anchovies, butter and vinegar into a small bowl and heat over a pan of boiling water, stirring frequently until you have a smooth brown cream. Arrange the fish on a warmed serving platter, pour over the anchovy sauce, sprinkle with the parsley and serve at once.

If you like anchovies, you'll love this recipe. The butter tends to smooth out the intensity of the very fishy flavour in the sauce, so that the cod has a chance to reveal its own taste. Any other white fish with a good firm texture will work equally well.

cod fillets with chilli, garlic and caper
pesce al peperoncino, aglio e capperi

SERVES 2

2 large fresh cod (or haddock) fillets
1 small onion, finely sliced
1 garlic clove, crushed
1 small handful of parsley, chopped
3 tablespoons olive oil
sea salt and freshly milled black pepper
½ tablespoon capers, drained, washed, dried and finely chopped
2 sardines, canned in olive oil
1 small potato, peeled and grated, drained in a sieve
4 tablespoons fish stock
½ dried red chilli pepper
juice of 1 lemon, strained
fresh herbs to garnish

Place the fish in a heavy-bottomed saucepan and cover with the onion, garlic, parsley and oil. Season with salt and pepper and cook gently for about 12 minutes. Remove the fish with a slotted spoon and keep warm on a platter.

Add the capers to the oil remaining in the pan. Trim and chop the sardines and add to the capers. Add the potato, stock and chilli, stir everything together and simmer for about 5 minutes.

Place the fish in the sauce and heat through for about 3 minutes. Remove the chilli and serve the fish and sauce on the platter, sprinkled with lemon juice and garnished with sprigs of herbs.

A lovely fish dish, with plenty of heat from the chillies and hints of delicious sharpness from the capers.

fish saltimbocca with pizzaiola sauce
saltimbocca di pesce con pizzaiola

SERVES 4

2 skinless monkfish tails,
    about 200 g (7 oz) each
4 thick slices mozzarella
4 large basil leaves
4 slices of Parma ham
3 garlic cloves
3 tablespoons extra virgin olive oil
200 ml (7 fl oz) passata
1 teaspoon dried oregano
sea salt and freshly milled
    black pepper

to garnish:
a handful of stoned green olives
sprigs of flat leaf parsley

Cut each piece of fish in half lengthways to create 4 equal pieces. Put the fish in a plastic bag and flatten it lightly with a mallet until reasonably thin but not torn.

Arrange the mozzarella on top of the fish, add a basil leaf and slice of Parma ham and secure with cocktail sticks.

Put half the olive oil in each of two separate frying pans. Put 1 whole peeled clove of garlic into one pan. Chop the remaining garlic and put it into the second pan. Heat the contents of both pans for about 2 minutes, then add the fish to the pan with the whole garlic and the passata to the other pan. Discard the whole garlic clove and cook the fish in the garlic-flavoured oil for about 3 minutes on each side; the mozzarella should just be starting to ooze. Stir the passata into the oil and garlic in the second pan and simmer briskly for about 5 minutes. Add the oregano and season to taste.

To serve, spoon a pool of the tomato sauce on to 4 individual plates and place a piece of fish on top. Remove the cocktail sticks. Garnish with a few green olives and a sprig of flat-leaf parsley, and serve at once.

saltimbocca — so delicious that it 'leaps in your mouth' — is traditionally made with veal and sage, but I have given it a fresh twist. Passata is made at the end of summer by sieving and bottling tomatoes to preserve them for winter. Here, I use them as a shortcut to make a simple tomato sauce.

chicken breasts with sun-dried tomatoes
petti di pollo con pomodori secchi

SERVES 4

4 large free-range chicken breasts
with skins

12 sun-dried tomatoes, drained,
oil reserved

150 g (5 oz) mozzarella, cut into
12 small strips

12 basil leaves, washed and dried

sea salt and freshly milled
black pepper

Preheat the oven to 180°C/350°F/gas mark 4. Trim the chicken breasts and cut a deep slash through the side of each breast, going about two thirds of the way in and across. Insert 3 sun-dried tomatoes into each slash, then add 3 slices of mozzarella and finally 3 basil leaves. Season with salt and pepper. Seal the breasts closed using a couple of wooden cocktail sticks.

Pour the oil from the jar of sun-dried tomatoes into an ovenproof dish large enough to hold the chicken. Place the chicken breasts in the oil and turn to coat them all over. Bake for about 45 minutes, basting frequently, until the chicken is golden brown and the mozzarella is oozing through. Serve with green beans, new potatoes and braised carrots.

The marvellous sweetness of sun-dried tomatoes complements the chicken and creates the summery flavour of this simple dish.

cold escalopes with tomatoes
cotolette fredde al pomodoro

SERVES 4

8 thin escalopes: veal, chicken,
   turkey, beef or pork
2 eggs, well beaten
a pinch of salt
4 tablespoons sunflower oil
6 tablespoons very fine dried
   white breadcrumbs
6 ripe tomatoes, deseeded
   and diced
a handful of fresh basil leaves,
   washed and dried
3 tablespoons extra virgin olive oil
sea salt and freshly milled
   black pepper

Trim the meat and flatten evenly with a meat mallet. Mix the eggs and salt in a shallow dish and immerse the escalopes in the mixture. Leave to stand for at least 2 hours.

Heat the sunflower oil in a wide frying pan. Put the breadcrumbs in a shallow dish. Taking a slice at a time, lift the meat from the egg mixture and allow most of the egg to drain back into the dish. Coat the meat evenly on both sides in the breadcrumbs, pressing down firmly so that the breadcrumbs adhere to the meat. Fry the breaded escalopes quickly in the hot oil, turning once or twice, making sure the meat is cooked through, crisp and golden. Drain thoroughly on kitchen paper and leave to cool.

Put the diced tomatoes into a colander and sprinkle with salt. Leave to drain over a bowl so that all excess water from the tomatoes seeps away. After 10 minutes or so, tip the drained tomatoes into a bowl and add the basil leaves, torn into shreds, the olive oil and freshly milled pepper. Mix well and top each escalope generously with the tomato and basil mixture. Arrange on a serving dish and decorate with sprigs of basil.

Cotolette are the Italian version of the classic Austrian dish, Wiener schnitzel. They are ideal for the hot summer when you need something light and easy to eat, either hot or cold. You can make them with veal, beef, pork, turkey, chicken or lamb and they are perfect with chunky chips and a green salad.

mascarpone ice cream
gelato al mascarpone

SERVES 4

400 g (14 oz) mascarpone
200 g (7 oz) icing sugar
4 egg yolks, beaten until pale

Beat all the ingredients together thoroughly. Pour into a plastic mould and freeze for at least 4 hours.

To this basic mixture you can add any of the following:
chopped candied fruits
chocolate chips
crumbled amaretti
grated lemon or orange zest
soft fruits or berries
chopped nougat or caramel

vanilla ice cream with amarena cherries
gelato all'amarena

SERVES 4

500 g best quality (preferably
  Italian!) rich vanilla ice cream
1 jar [450g] amarena cherries in
  syrup

Put the ice cream in your prettiest glass bowl and let it soften just enough so that it can be swirled into peaks. Spoon the cherries over it and serve immediately.

You can serve some amaretti biscuits alongside.

No ice cream has ever tasted as good as this treat I enjoyed as a child. Smooth velvety rich vanilla gelato is topped with these bitter-sweet cherries.

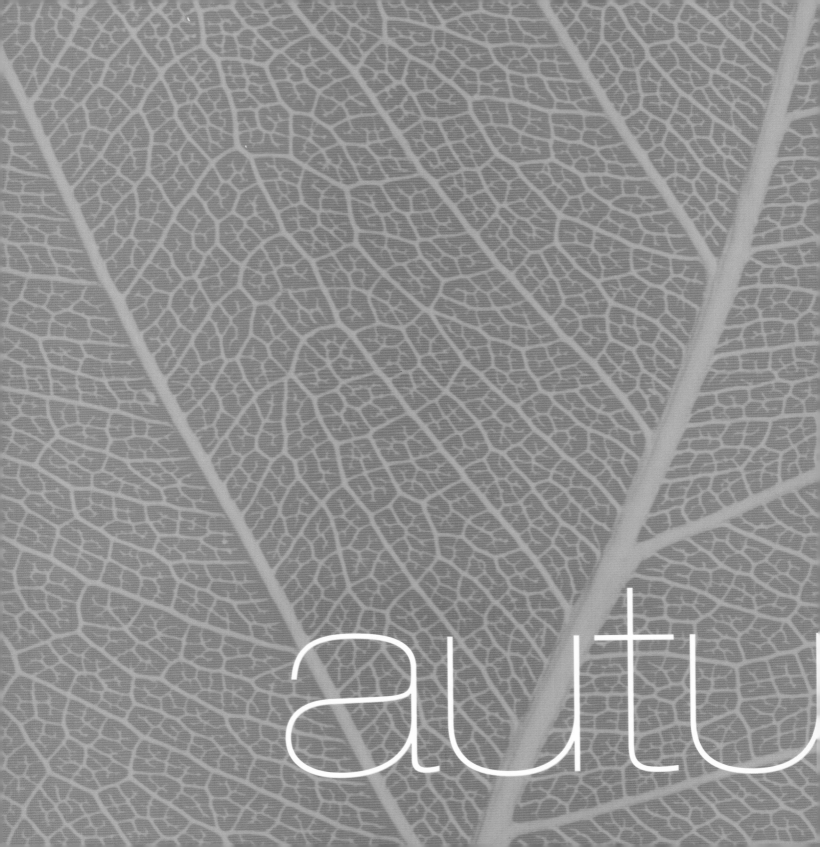

autumn preserves This is my favourite time of the year. Although the bounty of summer is drawing to a close, there is still, at the beginning of the season, a wealth of garden produce, resulting in a tremendous flurry of bottling and preserving activity which fills the days with unforgettable sights and smells.

It is as if each tomato bush, each pepper shrub and every stem of every vegetable plant is giving its all just now, making sure that each last second of warmth from the late summer sun is made to count. And despite the universal acceptance of freezers and microwaves, there is nothing to beat the ritual of gathering wild mushrooms by the basketload in the first of the chilly mornings, then preparing them for bottling under herb-laden olive oil. Or grilling what seems like a tonne of aubergines that will also end up in a neat row of jars on the shelf, or the pickling of peppers that have been roasted to rid them of their skins and scraped clean until they look like polished jewels.

All this happens every year among many of my friends and family, and the huge sense of satisfaction gained at the end of it all is worth every moment of effort. This is also the time for making jams and chutneys, and in some places it is also when the family pig is slaughtered so that it too can be preserved for the winter ahead. All this happens in those few weeks when summer and autumn are merging together, only to separate finally as the first frost falls and the buzz of mosquitoes and bees is replaced by the sparkling darkness of a cold night sky.

The second phase of autumn is when the olive harvest begins. Slowly, the groves are hung with wisps of blue smoke curling up into the steadily greying sky as the trees are pruned and the picking begins. In my part of Tuscany we only ever used the net method. This involves spreading huge nets on the grass under the trees and carefully drawing the olives down the branches by hand through your closed fist, letting your fingers uncurl at the last moment so that the fruit falls gently to the ground. When the net is covered with olives, the four corners are drawn together and the olives are picked over carefully to remove as much twig and leaf as possible, and then taken away to be pressed.

Any good olive oil producer will tell you that the picking is the most crucial part of the whole process of making fine olive oil. A bruised or split olive can begin to ferment very quickly and can turn the whole batch of oil rancid and unpalatable. Speed and care are of the essence, so that each and every olive reaches the press intact and perfect. The best producers manage the whole procedure, from branch to net to pressing, in about ninety minutes. The very first pressing of the oil, the green spurt caught on a piece of freshly baked bread held to the side of the barrel, is truly special and tastes better than anything I have ever known.

Once the olive trees have been stripped and pruned and left to rest through the winter, the game season begins in earnest. Wild boar, stewed for hours with wine and vegetables, provides the most delicious accompaniment for a golden slab of polenta made from the new season's maize, while the combination of pheasant with wild mushrooms is as fine a meal as anyone could wish for.

red pepper soup
minestra di peperoni rossi

SERVES 4

1 onion, sliced

3 garlic cloves, sliced

2 tablespoons extra virgin olive oil

2 large, juicy red peppers,
   thinly sliced

200 g (7 oz) canned tomatoes,
   drained

1 teaspoon Tabasco sauce

1 teaspoon dried mixed herbs

600 ml (1 pint) rich chicken or
   vegetable stock

200 ml (7 fl oz) crème fraîche

1 tablespoon lemon juice

½ teaspoon grated lemon zest

freshly milled black pepper

Fry the onion and garlic gently in the olive oil. As soon as the onion is soft, add the peppers and cook gently until they too are soft, then add the tomatoes, Tabasco and herbs. Add the stock and simmer for about 5 minutes.

Pour the mixture into a blender or food processor and blend briefly, keeping some of the pepper texture. Mix the crème fraîche, lemon juice and lemon zest together and season with pepper.

Reheat the soup to a very gentle simmer. Serve in bowls with some of the crème fraîche mixture spooned on top.

Alternatively, serve the soup chilled, adding the crème fraîche at the last moment.

Red peppers are so symbolic of early autumn days in Italy, especially in Piedmont. This is one of those lovely soups that is even better the day after you make it, and which can be eaten hot or cold.

roasted pepper salad
insalata di peperoni arrostiti

SERVES 2

2 juicy red peppers
2 garlic cloves, finely chopped
6 tablespoons olive oil
6 tablespoons chopped
   fresh parsley
sea salt and freshly milled
   black pepper

Place the peppers over a flame on the gas hob or under the grill and turn them until blackened all over. Put each pepper in a plastic bag and leave to cool completely.

Meanwhile, mix the garlic, olive oil and parsley together and season to taste. When the peppers are cooled, peel off the blackened skin, remove the seeds and membranes and slice the peppers into wide strips. Arrange the strips on a flat plate. Whisk the dressing and pour over. Leave to stand for at least 1 hour before serving.

stuffed peppers
peperoni ripieni

SERVES 4

4 very large green peppers or
   8 small ones

300g (11 oz) stale bread,
   crusts removed

600g (1¼ lb) canned tomatoes,
   deseeded and chopped

1 tablespoon capers (preferably
   salted), washed and chopped

50g (2 oz) green olives, stoned
   and sliced

fistful of fresh parsley, chopped

2 salted or 4 canned anchovy
   fillets, chopped

75g (3 oz) Pecorino cheese, grated

150 ml (5 fl oz) olive oil

sea salt and freshly milled
   black pepper

Wash and dry the peppers, remove the stems and carefully scoop out the seeds and membranes. Soften the bread in a little water, then mix in 3 chopped tomatoes and the capers, olives, parsley, anchovies, cheese and about 3 tablespoons of the oil. Mix well, season to taste, then spoon the mixture into the peppers.

Pour the remaining oil into an ovenproof dish just large enough to hold all the peppers and scatter the remaining tomatoes over the oil. Stand the peppers upright in the dish and bake for 1 hour in a low oven (150°C/300°F/gas mark 2) basting often with the tomato and oil sauce that will form around them. Serve hot or cold.

Yet another pepper recipe, because peppers abound in Italy's autumn like at no other time of the year! A lovely antipasto or an accompaniment to a simple grilled fish or chicken dish.

Italian sweet and sour onions
cipolle in agrodolce

SERVES 4

2 tablespoons sunflower oil

500 g (1 lb) button onions, peeled

3 tablespoons balsamic vinegar

1 tablespoon white wine vinegar

1 tablespoon sugar

sea salt and freshly milled
black pepper

Heat the oil in a wide, deep sauté pan and add the onions. Toss them in the hot oil until they begin to colour, then add the vinegars, sugar and seasoning. Stir and simmer uncovered until the acidic vinegar fumes have burned off, then add just enough water to barely cover and lower the heat. Cover the pan and simmer gently for about 30–40 minutes, stirring frequently, until the onions are tender and soft but not mushy.

If there is a lot of liquid left, take off the lid and raise the heat to boil away the excess. Serve hot or cold.

This is one of my favourite vegetable dishes, especially when made with the little flat button onions that you can buy in Italy already peeled and ready to use.

baked stuffed mushrooms
funghi ripieni al forno

SERVES 2

2 very large mushrooms or
　4 slightly smaller ones
3 tablespoons ricotta
1 tablespoon very soft Gorgonzola
2 tablespoons freshly grated
　Parmesan
2 tablespoons soft white
　breadcrumbs
1 tablespoon chopped fresh
　flat-leaf parsley
sea salt and freshly milled
　black pepper
3 tablespoons extra virgin olive oil

Preheat the oven to 180°C/350°F/gas mark 4.

Wipe the mushrooms clean and remove the stalks. Chop the stalks finely and place in a bowl. Add the ricotta, Gorgonzola, half the Parmesan, the breadcrumbs, parsley and salt and pepper to taste. Use the resulting mixture to fill the mushrooms generously.

Choose an ovenproof dish large enough for all the mushrooms to sit in flat, and brush with 1 tablespoon of olive oil. Put the filled mushrooms in the dish, drizzle the remaining oil over and around the mushrooms and bake for about 25 minutes, or until soft and golden brown on top. Serve at once.

parmesan and mushroom salad
insalata di funghi e parmigiano

SERVES 6

500 g (1 lb) fresh Parmesan cheese
500 g (1 lb) mushrooms, thinly sliced
juice of ½ lemon
2 tablespoons chopped fresh
　flat-leaf parsley
2 tablespoons olive oil
sea salt and freshly milled
　black pepper

Shave flakes of Parmesan off the wedge and cover the surface of six individual plates with cheese. Scatter the mushrooms on top so as almost to cover the cheese. Sprinkle each plate with lemon juice, parsley and olive oil and season to taste with salt and pepper. Leave to stand for 15 minutes before serving.

Choose the biggest and most flavourful mushrooms you can find for the recipes on page 94. Life is simply too busy to stuff individual, tiny mushrooms.

Autumn in Italy heralds the start of the porcini season and you can find huge fresh ones for sale on virtually every street vegetable stall; failing porcini, look for large, flattish field mushrooms.

pasta with green olive pâté and walnuts
pasta con crema di olive verdi e noci

SERVES 4

400 g (14 oz) conchiglie or fusilli
salt
1 small jar (190g) green olive pâté
100 g shelled walnuts, chopped
2–3 tablespoons extra virgin
   olive oil
100 g (3½ oz) Parmesan,
   freshly grated
3 tablespoons chopped fresh
   flat-leaf parsley

Bring a large saucepan of salted water to a rolling boil. Add the pasta and cook until tender. Drain thoroughly and return to the saucepan in which it was cooked.

Add the olive pâté and mix well, then add the walnuts, the olive oil and half the cheese. Mix again, then serve at once on warmed plates, sprinkled with the remaining Parmesan and the parsley.

November is still technically autumn in the kitchen as far as I am concerned, with winter beckoning all too speedily. This is when we get out into the olive groves and start the long, laborious task of harvesting. Although it will be a while before we can eat these freshly picked olives (they are too bitter until they have been processed) it is still time to celebrate and use olives in as many recipes as possible.

agnolotti or tortelloni with walnuts and mascarpone
agnolotti o tortelloni con noci e mascarpone

SERVES 4

50 g (2 oz) butter
100 g (3½ oz) mascarpone cheese
15 walnuts, shelled, peeled and
    coarsely chopped
400 g (14 oz) fresh agnolotti
    or tortelloni
50 g (2 oz) Parmesan,
    freshly grated
sea salt and freshly milled
    black pepper

Bring a large saucepan of salted water to a rolling boil.

Heat the butter in a small saucepan until melted but not browned. Mash the mascarpone with a fork until smooth, then stir in the walnuts.

Cook the pasta in the boiling water until tender. Drain thoroughly and return to the saucepan, pour over the melted butter and toss well. Add the walnut mixture and half the Parmesan and toss again. Season to taste, then sprinkle with the remaining Parmesan and serve at once in warmed bowls.

The abundance of nuts is so much a part of autumn for me that I wanted to share this recipe. It uses those pockets of pasta called either tortelloni or agnolotti depending upon their shape; they come with a variety of delicious fillings, such as duck, four cheese, asparagus, and the classic ricotta and spinach.

pasta with pancetta and mushrooms
pasta con pancetta e funghi

SERVES 4

125 g (4 oz) cubed pancetta or
   chopped bacon
200 g (7 oz) mushrooms, wiped
   clean and thinly sliced
2 tablespoons unsalted butter
1 garlic clove, finely chopped
3 tablespoons double cream
sea salt and freshly milled
   black pepper
400 g (14 oz) macaroni or other
   chunky pasta shape
50 g (2 oz) Parmesan,
   freshly grated
1 tablespoon finely chopped fresh
   flat-leaf parsley

Bring a large saucepan of salted water to a rolling boil.

In a heavy-bottomed frying pan over a low heat, cook the pancetta or
bacon until golden and crisp, and the fat runs – add a little olive oil only
if the bacon is sticking. Remove the bacon with a slotted spoon and
set aside. Add the mushrooms to the frying pan with the butter and
garlic and fry until the mushrooms are soft and well dried out. Stir in the
cream, season to taste and keep warm.

Meanwhile, boil the pasta until tender, then drain thoroughly and return
to the saucepan in which it was cooked. Pour the pancetta and the
mushroom and cream sauce over the pasta and toss together, then
add half the Parmesan and toss again. Serve at once on warmed
plates, sprinkled with the rest of the Parmesan and the parsley.

*A filling, substantial dish to feed
the hungry after working on those 'bedding
down for winter' jobs.*

aubergine and mozzarella lasagne
lasagne di melanzane e mozzarella

SERVES 4

1 large aubergine, cubed

2 garlic cloves, finely chopped

6 tablespoons olive oil

2 x 400 g (14 oz) cans chopped
tomatoes

sea salt and freshly milled
black pepper

10 fresh basil leaves, torn
into pieces

500 ml (16 fl oz) béchamel sauce

350 g (13 oz) dried lasagne verdi

8 tablespoons freshly grated
Parmesan

150 g (5 oz) mozzarella, cubed

Preheat the oven to 180°C/350°F/gas mark 4.

Fry the aubergine and garlic in half the olive oil for about 5 minutes, or until browned and softened slightly. Add the tomatoes and simmer for about 10 minutes. Season to taste, then add the basil.

Cover the bottom of an ovenproof dish with about a third of the béchamel. Arrange a layer of lasagne on top. Cover the lasagne with half the aubergine sauce, then add a sprinkling of Parmesan and a few cubes of mozzarella. Repeat the layers and finish with the remaining béchamel. Cover loosely with foil and bake for about 25 minutes, then remove the foil and raise the heat to allow the lasagne to brown.

Leave to stand for 5 minutes before serving.

Few things are more satisfying than a generous wedge of lasagne after you've finished sweeping leaves off the lawn. You are allowed to cheat and use ready-made béchamel if you feel so inclined: after all, you've spent so much energy on the leaf sweeping!

seared scallops with rosemary and lemon
capesante con rosmarino e limone

SERVES 2

2 teaspoons finely chopped
   fresh rosemary
1 garlic clove, very finely chopped
4 tablespoons extra virgin olive oil
fine sea salt and freshly milled
   black pepper
6 large scallops, cleaned and
   ready to cook
1 small lemon, halved

Mix the rosemary, garlic, olive oil, salt and pepper in a shallow bowl, add the scallops and leave to stand for a few minutes.

Heat a heavy-bottomed frying pan or griddle pan and brush a mere smudge of oil over the surface. When the pan is really hot, add the scallops and cook very quickly, 1–2 minutes on each side, squeezing over the lemon juice as they cook. Transfer to a warmed serving dish.

Pour any remaining marinade and lemon juice into the pan. Swirl it all around, scraping the bottom of the pan with a wooden spoon to dislodge any residue, and then pour it all, bubbling hot, over the cooked scallops. Serve at once.

Choose nice big scallops, which will cope best with being quickly seared over a very high heat. You could also use flattened chunks of monkfish. Serve with chunky chips and a green salad. A yummy autumn lunchtime treat.

judith's seared scallop and fennel salad
insalata di capesante e finocchio di giudita

SERVES 6

1 small red onion, finely sliced

1 small fennel bulb, finely sliced

a large handful of rocket, washed
 and dried

a large handful of watercress,
 washed and dried

1 little gem lettuce, leaves
 separated, washed and dried

1 teaspoon extra virgin olive oil

12 large fresh scallops, cleaned
 and ready to cook

for the omelette:

3 egg whites

pinch of salt

pinch of sugar

1 teaspoon extra virgin olive oil

a little vegetable oil for frying

for the dressing:

4 tablespoons lemon juice

4 tablespoons orange juice

2 teaspoons horseradish cream

sea salt and freshly milled
 black pepper

Whisk all the dressing ingredients together in a small bowl.

To make the omelette: whisk together the egg whites, salt, sugar and olive oil. Heat a little vegetable oil in a non-stick frying pan. Pour in half the omelette mixture. Cook briefly, on one side only, until the mixture is just set. Turn out and repeat with the remaining mixture. Roll up and slice finely to make narrow shreds.

Combine the omelette with the onion, fennel and salad leaves.

Heat a heavy-bottomed frying pan until searing hot, add the olive oil and the scallops and sear very briefly on both sides: do not overcook or they will toughen.

Add just enough dressing to the salad to moisten the leaves, without drenching them. Pile the salad on to individual plates with the scallops on top and serve at once.

A sophisticated salad for a dinner party, but simplicity itself to prepare. Omit the omelette if you are short of time or energy. This recipe belongs to my dear friend and cooking partner Judith Sweet, who lives in Tasmania, where all the seasons are back to front!

chicken breasts with a pepper and goat's cheese sauce
petti di pollo con salsina di peperoni e caprino

SERVES 2

2 chicken breasts, boned but with
   the skin left on
2 thin slices of Parma ham
¼ teaspoon dried thyme or 2 large
   sprigs fresh thyme
2 garlic cloves, thinly sliced
3 tablespoons soft goat's cheese,
   such as Caprino
3 tablespoons extra virgin olive oil
1 large red or yellow pepper,
   deseeded and sliced into strips
4 tablespoons chicken stock
sea salt and freshly milled
   black pepper
a large handful of fresh basil
   leaves, torn into small pieces

Make a slit down the side of each chicken breast to make a pocket. Tuck a slice of Parma ham inside each breast. Add the thyme, half the garlic and half the cheese. Close the pockets of chicken and secure using wooden cocktail sticks.

Heat half the oil in a frying pan until sizzling. Add the chicken, skin side down, and fry for about 5 minutes, then turn and fry on the other side for a further 2 minutes. Add the rest of the garlic and the pepper strips. Pour over the stock and season to taste. Reduce the heat, cover and simmer for about 5 minutes, or until the peppers are soft and the chicken is cooked through.

Take the chicken out of the pan and keep warm. Add the remaining cheese to the pan. Either use a hand-held blender or tip the contents of the pan into a blender or food processor and blend until completely smooth. Divide the sauce between two warmed plates, place the chicken on top and serve at once, sprinkled with basil.

Yellow or red peppers can be used for this surprisingly simple chicken dish. A hand-held blender makes short work of the sauce.

duck breasts with red onion and balsamic vinegar

petto d'anatra con cipolla rossa e aceto balsamico

SERVES 2

2 duck breasts, boned but with
skin left on
2 teaspoons sunflower oil
1 large red onion, thinly sliced
1 teaspoon unrefined caster sugar
sea salt and freshly milled
black pepper
2 teaspoons balsamic vinegar
4 teaspoons finely snipped chives

Trim the duck breasts, wash and pat dry. Heat the oil in a heavy-bottomed frying pan until sizzling hot, then lay the duck breasts in the hot oil, skin side down. Do not move or turn the duck breasts but leave them to sizzle, shaking the pan from time to time, for about 6 minutes, then turn over and repeat. Take the breasts out of the pan and keep warm.

Add the onion to the pan and moisten with a spoonful or two of water. Sprinkle with the sugar, salt and pepper and let the onions cook over a medium heat, stirring frequently, until soft and caramelized. Add the balsamic vinegar and return the duck to the pan. Reheat for about 4 minutes, turning the duck twice. Serve at once, sprinkled with the chives.

A rich and filling dish, perfect for supper on a chilly evening. Serve with a slightly tart salad, perhaps with citrus fruits or watercress, to cleanse the palate and refresh the mouth.

beef fillet with red peppers
filetto ai peperoni

SERVES 2

3 tablespoons extra virgin olive oil
1 small onion, thinly sliced
2 sticks of celery, trimmed and
    coarsely chopped
1 large red pepper, deseeded and
    thinly sliced
1 little gem lettuce, finely chopped
1 tablespoon unsalted butter
2 thick fillet steaks, trimmed
1 small glass of Marsala wine
sea salt and freshly milled
    black pepper

Put the olive oil, onion, celery and pepper into a frying pan. Cook gently until the onion is well softened, then add the lettuce and continue to cook for 2–3 minutes. Using a slotted spoon, remove all the vegetables and put them to one side.

Add the butter to the pan and turn up the heat slightly. When it is sizzling, add the steaks and cook for about 3 minutes on each side. Remove the meat from the pan and add it to the reserved vegetables.

Pour the Marsala into the pan and stir thoroughly to detach any residue from the bottom of the pan. Drain in any juices that may have seeped out from the vegetables and meat and allow to bubble together for 1 minute.

Return the vegetables and meat to the pan to reheat for no more than 2 minutes over a high heat; season to taste, then serve at once on warmed plates.

Italian markets are flooded with boxes and boxes of multicoloured peppers during the autumn months, ready for bottling and pickling. In this recipe the sweetness of the peppers is heightened by the meat juices and the Marsala. If you wish, you can blanch the pepper in boiling water to loosen the fine outer skin, then slip the skin off before de-seeding and slicing the pepper into strips.

veal escalope with walnuts
scaloppina di vitello alle noci

SERVES 2

50 g (2 oz) butter
25 g (1 oz) walnuts (fresh, slightly
    soft walnuts are best)
250 g (9 oz) veal escalopes,
    pounded with a meat mallet until
    very thin
2 tablespoons plain white flour
sea salt and freshly milled
    black pepper
4 tablespoons dry white wine

Melt half the butter in a frying pan, add the walnuts and fry very gently for about 10 minutes, turning frequently. Then process them coarsely and set aside.

Add the remaining butter to the pan and lightly coat the veal in flour. Fry the escalopes in the hot butter for about 2 minutes on each side, until the meat is just cooked and golden brown. Season and remove the meat, keeping it warm.

Pour the wine into the pan and stir thoroughly to detach the residue from the bottom of the pan, add the walnuts and mix together, then return the meat to the pan and turn the pieces over two or three times to coat them thoroughly. Serve the meat on a warmed platter and pour over the cooking juices from the pan.

The autumn always puts me in the mood for eating nuts of all different types, shapes and sizes. This recipe is also delicious with hazelnuts.

sausages with cannellini beans
salsicce con fagioli cannellini

SERVES 4, GENEROUSLY

4 teacups dried white cannellini
   beans, soaked overnight in cold
   water (or 2 x 400 g/14 oz cans of
   cannellini beans, drained)
6 garlic cloves, crushed
8 Italian or coarse pork sausages
4 tablespoons olive oil
1 sprig rosemary
1 heaped tablespoon tomato purée
sea salt and freshly milled
   black pepper

Rinse the soaked beans and boil them in fresh water very fast for about 5 minutes, then drain and rinse again. Place in another saucepan and cover with plenty of fresh water. Simmer until tender.

Add half the garlic and all the sausages. Continue to simmer until the sausages are cooked through and the beans are also cooked, about 20 minutes.

Heat the oil in a frying pan, add the rosemary, tomato purée and remaining garlic and fry for about 5 minutes, then add the sausages and brown them all over. Finally, add the beans and stir together thoroughly. Season with salt and pepper and simmer until bubbling hot. Serve drizzled with a little olive oil.

High up on my 'naughty but nice' list are those deliciously peppery, incredibly juicy, fatty Italian sausages that are later hung up to dry out and magically become salami. Autumn and winter are the best times to indulge in their intense flavour and superb texture. On sunny autumn days, when we are out pruning the olive trees and the orchards, we make bonfires of the prunings and arrange the sausages on long sticks in a circle around the fire. The stick is thrust through the sausage lengthways, so the fat drains downwards into the ground instead of into our arteries!

How well I remember the arrival of the first baskets of wild mirtilli. These tiny blue-black berries grow close to the ground, hugging the soil tightly. The locals pick them with a pettine da mirtillo, a long-toothed metal comb on the end of a long handle with which they painstakingly scrape the sides of the mountains where the mirtilli grow – uphill of course, so that the berries fall towards the picker! I use mirtilli, berries with the most fabulous flavour, in this impressive-looking dessert; it's incredibly easy to make, but you do need to freeze it well in advance. If mirtilli are unavailable, use blackberries, raspberries or strawberries. Frozen berries are also acceptable.

blueberry semifreddo
semifreddo di mirtilli

SERVES 6–8

225 g (8 oz) blueberries, washed
    and hulled
3 tablespoons sweet fruit liqueur,
    such as cherry brandy
300 ml (10 fl oz) double cream
4 tablespoons mascarpone
75 g (3 oz) icing sugar, sifted
125 g (4 oz) crushed meringues

for the sauce :
225 g (8 oz) blueberries, washed
    and hulled
2 tablespoons caster sugar

to decorate :
a few blueberries
sprigs of mint or edible flowers

Line a 20 cm (8 inch) diameter spring-form cake tin with baking parchment.

Puree the berries in a blender or food processor. If you like, rub through a sieve to remove the seeds. Stir in the liqueur.

Whip the cream with the mascarpone and icing sugar and fold in the meringues. Fold this mixture into the blueberry puree, then pour into the cake tin. Freeze for 6 hours.

Meanwhile, make the sauce: put the blueberries and sugar into a small saucepan and simmer until soft, stirring frequently. Push this mixture through a food mill or a sieve and chill until required.

To serve: invert the cake tin onto a very cold plate, remove the paper and slice the semifreddo into 6 or 8 wedges. Serve with a little pool of sauce, scatter with a few extra berries and add a sprig of mint or a few edible flowers.

amaretto semifreddo
semifreddo all'amaretto

SERVES 2

3 egg yolks
2 tablespoons caster sugar
3 tablespoons Amaretto liqueur
4 large amaretti biscuits, crumbled
125 ml (4 fl oz) double cream,
    whisked until just peaking

Beat the egg yolks until very pale, then beat in the sugar. Add the liqueur and the amaretti and gently stir together.

Fold in the cream and transfer the mixture into freezer-safe glasses. Freeze until only just solidifying (about 2 hours), then serve.

apples with honey and grappa
mele con miele e grappa

SERVES 2

3 tablespoons melted butter

2 large eating apples, if possible russets

2–3 tablespoons Grappa

2 tablespoons clear honey

Put a large heavy-bottomed non-stick frying pan over a medium heat and brush lightly with a little melted butter.

Meanwhile, core the apples, then slice each apple into 6 rings. Brush the rings with melted butter and lay them in the pan. Cook for 2–3 minutes on each side, or until lightly browned and softened. Pour over the Grappa and allow to flame briefly to burn off the alcohol. Remove the apples from the pan and keep them warm.

Add the honey to the pan and heat through until bubbling hot, stirring it into the apple and Grappa residue. Pour the honey over the hot apples and serve at once with cream or ice cream.

The autumn chills bring with them the start of the apple season. My favourite apples are called ranuncola in Italy – at least, the market traders in Via Metauro always used that name for slightly squat, rounded red apples with a streaked effect on the skin. I remember going to the market for fruit on those freezing mornings and being amazed at the way the traders used old newspapers to line their clothes in order to keep warm.

MiLLE
Foglie
£ 7500

GALLE
COTTE AL
FORNO
£ 2000

PANE con
Fichi
£ 900

PANE
con UVA
£ 900

CANNOLi
£ 1200

PANE
GRECO

italian apple cake
torta di mele

SERVES 6

2 oz (50g) butter, cut into small pieces, plus extra for greasing

3 tablespoons stale breadcrumbs

2 large eggs

5 oz (150 g) caster sugar

6½ oz (185 g) plain white flour, sifted

4 fl oz (120 ml) milk

grated rind of ½ lemon

1 heaped teaspoon baking powder, sifted

2lb (1 kg) apples (any sort except Bramley) peeled and thinly sliced

2 oz (50 g) butter

2 tablespoons granulated or light brown sugar

Preheat the oven to 180°C/350°F/gas mark 4. Butter a 10 inch (25 cm) cake tin thoroughly, then dust with the breadcrumbs. Turn the tin upside down and discard the loose breadcrumbs.

Beat the eggs until light and fluffy, adding the caster sugar gradually, then fold in the flour, milk, lemon rind and baking powder. The mixture should be quite runny. Pour the mixture into the cake tin, then arrange the apples on top, dot with the butter, sprinkle with the granulated or light brown sugar and bake for 55 minutes. Leave in the tin to cool completely before removing.

My children, who are an almost perfect combination of Anglo-Italian when it comes to eating habits, like to slather great wedges of this cake with gallons of homemade, creamy, eggy and very very English custard. And when I am not there to make the custard, they just open a tin...

persimmon sciaciatta
sciaciatta di caki

SERVES 6

8 large, ripe persimmons, peeled
   and stoned
12 tablespoons granulated sugar
oil for greasing

for the dough:
25 g (1 oz) fresh yeast
200 ml (7 fl oz) warm water
400 g (14 oz) strong plain
   white flour
a pinch of salt
2–3 teaspoons olive oil

To make the dough, mix the yeast and water together and add about 2 tablespoons of the flour. Put this mixture in a warm place to rise for about 30 minutes.

Sift the rest of the flour on to a work surface. Knead the yeast mixture thoroughly, then knead it into the flour, adding a little more water if necessary. Add the salt and oil and knead energetically for about 10 minutes. Transfer this mixture to a large floured bowl and leave in a warm place to rise for about 1 hour or until doubled in size.

Preheat the oven to 220°C/425°F/gas mark 7.

Roll out the dough to a large circle and place on a well-oiled baking sheet. Sprinkle the dough with a little oil and then cover the surface with the persimmons, pressing them down into the dough. Sprinkle with the sugar, then bake for about 15–20 minutes, or until the dough has risen and the fruit has caramelized with the sugar. Sprinkle with a little more sugar and serve warm or cold.

Traditionally, this would be made using grapes, but I love persimmons and for me they are also very much a part of autumn. In the spring, I sometimes use loquats instead, putting them on top of the dough in exactly the same way, peeled and stoned. If you cannot be bothered to make your own dough, try using a good-quality bread or pizza dough mix.

erno winter

winter spices

As I am by nature incredibly impatient, I have always detested the winter months, with the exception of Christmas, which I adore, and Carnevale. Winter in Italy, when I was a child, meant darkness that came all too early in the day, and plenty of hot, comforting food to chase away the draughts and make this long period of what has always felt to me like a long and unnecessary wait, more bearable.

In terms of culinary treats, it is not all bad. Winter time gives me licence to use ingredients that have not been used for some months, indeed since the previous winter. Spices come into their own to warm and cheer, and dried fruits can be used in all manner of ways. This too is the time for hearty, rib-sticking stews of pork, beef and the stringier, older game; for delicious, colourful soups and mounds of fluffy mashed potato with which to soak up the juices on the plate; and, most of all, for polenta.

Now as far as this porridge of ground maize, water and salt is concerned, I know I will have to be very persuasive indeed to get you to enjoy, as I did so often as a child, the pleasure of spooning up a bowl of freshly cooked, slightly soft polenta covered in hot milk with a knob of butter. Curled up on a window sill with a book, watching the rain sheeting down outside, this winter treat has seen me through many a long and tedious hour, but it can be eaten in many other ways. One of the best is layered in slices with a tomato-laden meat stew nestling in between the layers and a generous topping of mozzarella and Parmesan. Or you can have a slab of it, fresh cooked or grilled or fried, alongside a rich red wine casserole of wild boar or other meat that needs a long, slow cooking time.

Winter is also the time for cardoons, boiled and sliced, then covered with a layer of Taleggio or Fontina cheese and baked until the cheese melts and bubbles. Or puréed and turned into a creamy soup into which hunks of coarse country bread can be dunked.

In terms of fruit, there was always a plethora of citrus fruits with their brilliantly coloured skins to brighten up the table. From the early mandarins to the huge globes of the later oranges, we never had a shortage of vitamin C in my Italian childhood. The smaller, less impressive-looking fruits were squeezed for fresh juice at breakfast time.

Christmas Day was always interesting in our household, as we managed to combine English and Italian traditions. On Christmas Eve, after Midnight Mass and the subsequent fish feast, pillow cases would be parked with hope at the foot of our beds. On the following morning, we would begin the day with a fantastic breakfast: blood oranges squeezed into tall, frosted glasses, and big bowls of caffe latte into which we could dunk great chunks of Panettone spread thickly with apricot jam. After that, and the opening of the presents, it was all hands on deck for the big roast turkey and Christmas pudding number which would be served about 3 o'clock in the afternoon, complete with imported crackers.

Long walks in the pale winter sunshine would then prepare us for the feast of St Stephen, or Boxing Day, when all friends and family would gather for the day-long buffet. But even all these delights, and the glorious, table-groaning feasts of the Christmas period, and the delicious fried pastries made to celebrate Carnevale, could not stop me longing for the first warm days of spring. To me the winter was a time when I felt irritated, cooped up indoors and starved of sunshine and heat. Each passing day of grey brought closer the arrival of spring and all her gifts.

lentil and apple soup
minestra di lenticchie e mele

SERVES 4

150 g (5 oz) brown or green lentils

5 tablespoons olive oil

1 stick of celery, chopped

1 large carrot, chopped

1 large onion, chopped

2 garlic cloves chopped

3 rashers pancetta or streaky
   bacon, chopped (optional)

small sprig of rosemary

4 or 5 apples, peeled and cubed

250 ml (8 fl oz) chicken or
   meat stock

sea salt and freshly milled
   black pepper

Soak the lentils overnight in plenty of cold water.

The following day, drain and rinse them and place them in a saucepan with fresh water to cover. Bring to the boil and boil for 5 minutes, then drain and rinse again. Return to the pan, and just cover with fresh cold water. Simmer for about 15 minutes.

In a separate pan, heat the olive oil and add the celery, carrot, onion, garlic, bacon and rosemary. Fry gently until the fat in the bacon begins to run. Add the lentils with all their liquid, stir, season generously and cover. Simmer slowly for about 30 minutes, stirring frequently.

Add the apples and stock and simmer, uncovered, until the apples are tender. Taste and adjust the seasoning and serve at once, with bread and salad. Also excellent served cold.

This is one of my favourite easy-to-eat meals. Ideal in winter or summer, it is a very cheap and nourishing way to feed a family ... deliciously!

chestnut and porcini mushroom soup
minestra di castagne e porcini

SERVES 4

1 shallot, chopped very finely

2 tablespoons unsalted butter

a large handful of dried porcini
mushrooms, soaked in warm
water to cover

350 g (13 oz) peeled cooked
chestnuts

750 ml (1¼ pints) flavourful
vegetable or chicken stock

sea salt and freshly milled
black pepper

3 tablespoons chopped fresh
flat-leaf parsley

Fry the shallot in the butter very gently until it is softened and golden brown.

Drain the mushrooms and reserve; strain the liquid carefully through a double sheet of kitchen paper. Chop the mushrooms coarsely and add to the shallots. Stir together for a few minutes, then add the liquid from the mushrooms and the chestnuts, the stock and salt and pepper to taste. Simmer very gently, stirring occasionally until the soup begins to thicken. Stir through the parsley and serve hot.

A lovely brown and creamy soup with the two very wintry flavours of dried porcini mushrooms and chestnuts. Soothing and comforting, yet quite luscious in both texture and flavour, this is a magnificent soup.

tuscan vegetable soup
la ribollita

SERVES 4, GENEROUSLY

250 g (9 oz) stale country style
   white or brown bread, the staler
   the better
2 tablespoons olive oil, plus extra
   to serve
sea salt and freshly milled
   black pepper
3 carrots, chopped coarsely
2 medium potatoes, peeled
   and cubed
2 garlic cloves, finely chopped
2 onions, finely sliced
1 small cabbage, shredded
4 Italian sausages
125 g (4 oz) cooked cannellini
   beans

Slice the bread, brush it thoroughly on both sides with olive oil and season with salt and pepper. Use it to line a soup tureen or large bowl.

Put all the vegetables and the sausages into a large saucepan and cover with about 1.2 litres (2 pints) cold water. Season with salt and pepper, cover and simmer for about 1 hour and 30 minutes, stirring occasionally and adding more water if required.

Remove the sausages and keep warm. Stir the beans into the soup and simmer for a further 10 minutes. Taste and adjust the seasoning, then pour the soup over the bread in the tureen or bowl. Arrange the sausages on top, then cover and leave to rest for about 10 minutes before serving. Offer a small jug of olive oil so that people can drizzle it over their individual portions as they want to. You can also offer grated Parmesan.

Since my initiation to this recipe by my old friend and confidant Alvaro Maccioni, of La Famiglia restaurant in London, I have come across many other versions of this great Tuscan classic.

chilli and cauliflower soup
minestra di cavolfiore con peperoncino

SERVES 6

1 medium cauliflower, quartered
1.2 litres (2 pints) vegetable stock
sea salt
4 garlic cloves, peeled
1 dried red chilli pepper
4 tablespoons olive oil

to serve:
2–3 tablespoons extra virgin
   olive oil
freshly grated pecorino cheese

Boil the cauliflower in the stock with 2 pinches of salt until tender.

Meanwhile, fry the garlic and chilli in the olive oil until the garlic is golden.

Drain the cauliflower and reserve the stock. Chop the cauliflower quite coarsely and add to the saucepan with the garlic; fry gently together until the cauliflower has fallen to pieces completely and is soft and oily.

Add the stock in which the cauliflower was cooked and simmer gently until the soup is more or less smooth. Discard the garlic and chilli. Transfer to a soup tureen or individual bowls, lined with toasted bread rubbed with garlic and drizzled with chilli oil. Drizzle the surface of the soup with a little olive oil or chilli oil and sprinkle generously with grated pecorino cheese just before serving.

This is a very warming soup,
and an excellent dish for chilly
winter evenings!

cauliflower cheese with parma ham
gratin di cavolfiore con prosciutto crudo

SERVES 2

1 small cauliflower. trimmed, cored,
   and quartered
pinch of freshly grated nutmeg,
   mace or cinnamon
75 g (3 oz) freshly grated Parmesan
50 g (2 oz) lean Parma ham,
   cut into thin strips
50 g (2 oz) Taleggio or fontina
   cheese, cubed
sea salt and freshly milled
   black pepper

for the béchamel sauce:
25 g (1 oz) unsalted butter
25 g (1 oz) plain white flour
300 ml (10 fl oz) milk

Preheat the oven to gas mark 4/350°F/180°C.

Drop the cauliflower quarters into a saucepan of simmering salted water and cook until just tender. Drain thoroughly and transfer to an ovenproof dish.

For the sauce, melt the butter in a saucepan until foaming, then add the flour and whisk vigorously to make a smooth, lump-free paste. Add the milk and whisk together thoroughly. Stir until thickened enough to coat the back of a spoon and until the sauce no longer has a floury flavour.

Remove from the heat and stir in the spice, half the Parmesan, the Parma ham and the fontina or Taleggio. Season to taste. Pour over the cauliflower, sprinkle with the remaining Parmesan and bake for about 15 minutes. Serve with crusty bread and salad.

A simple, comforting supper dish for two on a cold winter's evening, with just a hint of sophistication thanks to the delicious cheese combination and the slivers of Parma ham!

ham and egg tartlets
tartine di prosciutto e uova

SERVES 6

150 g (5 oz) Parma ham,
150 g (5 oz) fresh ciabatta or
   focaccia breadcrumbs
a good pinch of grated nutmeg
sea salt and freshly milled
   black pepper
75 ml (3 fl oz) milk
50 g (2 oz) butter
3 tablespoons dry breadcrumbs
6 eggs

Preheat the oven to 180°C/350°F/gas mark 4.

Chop the ham finely and mix together with the breadcrumbs. Add a generous pinch of nutmeg and season well. Add enough milk to make a thick paste.

Butter six 6–8 cm (2½–3 inch) patty tins and coat thickly with dry breadcrumbs. Divide the ham mixture between the six tins. Break an egg carefully into each one, sprinkle lightly with more dry breadcrumbs and dot with butter. Bake for about 15 minutes. Remove carefully from the tins and serve hot with a small green salad.

rice salad with bresaola
insalata di riso con bresaola

SERVES 6

300 g (11 oz) long-grain rice, boiled,
   drained and rinsed
200 g (7 oz) bresaola
a handful of black olives, stoned
   and coarsely chopped
½ tablespoon capers, chopped
2 ripe plum tomatoes, thinly sliced
3 spring onions, chopped
3 tablespoons olive oil
1 tablespoon white wine vinegar
sea salt and freshly milled
   black pepper

Rinse and chop the capers and snip the bresaola into small strips. Mix the rice, bresaola, olives, capers, tomatoes and spring onions together in a bowl. Mix the oil and vinegar together and season to taste with salt and pepper. Pour the dressing over the salad ingredients and toss thoroughly. Leave to stand for about 1 hour before serving.

baked polenta
polenta al forno

SERVES 6

2 onions, finely chopped
1 garlic clove, finely chopped
1 stick of celery, chopped
1 carrot, chopped
4 tablespoons olive oil
500 ml (16 fl oz) passata
1 bay leaf
sea salt and freshly milled
   black pepper
400 g (14 oz) cooked polenta,
   cut into neat slices
300 g (11 oz) mozzarella, cubed
300 g (11 oz) mushrooms, sautéed
200 g (7 oz) Parmesan, grated
3 tablespoons extra virgin olive oil

Fry the onions, garlic, celery and carrot in the olive oil until the vegetables are soft. Add the passata and the bay leaf, season and simmer gently for about 45 minutes.

Preheat the oven to 190°C/375°F/gas mark 5.

Oil an ovenproof dish and arrange a layer of polenta on the bottom. Cover with a thin layer of the sauce, then sprinkle with cubed mozzarella, a layer of mushrooms and one of grated Parmesan. Drizzle with a little extra virgin olive oil, then repeat the layers until all the sauce and the cheese has been used up. If you have some polenta left over, grill it separately and drizzle it with a little oil. You can eat this while you wait for the main dish! Bake the layered polenta for about 30 minutes. Serve piping hot.

This is a very filling dish, so to follow I would recommend nothing more than a plate of refreshing salad!

grilled polenta with sauteed mushrooms and melted cheese
polenta alla griglia con funghi e formaggio

SERVES 4

8 slices of cooked polenta, about
    10 x 5 cm (4 x 2 inches) each
3 tablespoons olive oil, plus a little
    extra for brushing
250 g (9 oz) fontina or Asiago
    cheese, cubed
about 150 ml (5 fl oz) milk
400 g (14 oz) mushrooms,
    thinly sliced
2 garlic cloves, thinly sliced
sea salt and freshly milled
    black pepper
3 tablespoons finely chopped fresh
    flat-leaf parsley

Preheat the grill and brush the polenta slices lightly with oil.

Meanwhile, put the cheese in a small saucepan with just enough milk to cover the cheese. Place this over a larger pan of simmering water to melt the cheese and blend it with the milk, stirring frequently.

While the cheese is melting, cook the mushrooms and garlic in the olive oil in a frying pan, stirring frequently for about 10 minutes. Season to taste.

When the cheese and milk have formed a smooth sauce, grill the polenta on both sides. Serve 2 slices of polenta per person, cover with some of the melted cheese and scatter the mushrooms on top. Sprinkle with parsley and serve at once.

You can vary the flavour by using fried onions instead of mushrooms if you prefer.

baked semolina gnocchi
gnocchi di semolino al forno

SERVES 6

1 litre (1¾ pints) milk
250 g (9 oz) semolina
2 egg yolks
125 g (4 oz) Parmesan, grated
125 g (4 oz) unsalted butter
a pinch of ground cinnamon
sea salt and freshly milled
    black pepper

Preheat the oven to 220°C/425°F/gas mark 7.

Bring the milk to the boil in a large saucepan. Sprinkle in the semolina with one hand so that it falls into the water like a fine rain, whisking constantly to prevent lumps. Continue whisking until the mixture begins to thicken, then use a wooden spoon to stir constantly for about 10 minutes, as the semolina cooks through. It is ready when it comes away from the bottom of the pan and forms a smooth ball. Remove from the heat, stir in the egg yolks, half the Parmesan and half the butter and season to taste with cinnamon, salt and pepper.

Dampen a work surface lightly with cold water and spread the semolina out flat, about 1 cm (½ inch) thick, with a wide-bladed knife dipped in cold water.

Using a pastry cutter, cut the semolina into small circles. Use some of the remaining butter to grease a shallow ovenproof dish. Arrange a layer of gnocchi on the bottom, cover with a little Parmesan and a few dots of butter. Repeat until all the ingredients have been used up. Melt any remaining butter and trickle it over the top. Bake for about 15 minutes and serve hot.

This is one of the most comforting of all the winter recipes that I remember from my childhood. You may like to add a little powdered saffron to the semolina, or you can vary the cheeses you decide to use.

baked pasta with mackerel and tomato
pasta al forno con sgombri e pomodoro

SERVES 4 –6

500 g (1 lb) macaroni

sea salt and freshly milled
 black pepper

5 tablespoons extra virgin olive oil,
 plus extra for greasing

300 g (11 oz) mackerel fillets,
 skinned

2 garlic cloves, finely chopped

400 g (14 oz) canned tomatoes,
 chopped

1 tablespoon capers, rinsed
 and chopped

2 tablespoons black olives, stoned

1 teaspoon dried oregano

250 g (9 oz) mozzarella,
 finely chopped

2 tablespoons fresh breadcrumbs

Preheat the oven to 190°C/375°F/gas mark 5.

Bring a large pot of salted water to a rolling boil. Cook the pasta in the boiling water until tender, then drain and rinse briefly under cold running water; drain well. Transfer the pasta into a large mixing bowl and add 2 tablespoons olive oil. Stir to coat the pasta and set aside.

Cut the fish into cubes and rinse under cold running water, then pat dry. Heat the remaining oil in a saucepan, add the garlic and fry for about 4 minutes, then add the fish and stir briefly to coat the fish in the oil and garlic. Add the tomatoes and stir well. Simmer for about 10 minutes, stirring frequently. Add the capers, olives and oregano, taste and adjust the seasoning and simmer for a further 10 minutes.

Pour this sauce over the pasta and mix well. Transfer to an oiled ovenproof dish and level the top. Sprinkle the mozzarella over the surface and then sprinkle with the breadcrumbs. Drizzle with the rest of the oil and bake for about 25 minutes or until heated through and well browned on top. Serve at once.

Deliciously filling, using a fish that I always associate with the wintertime.

baked mackerel fillets
pesce azzuro al forno

SERVES 2

4 mackerel fillets, about 400–500 g
(14 oz–1 lb)
4 tablespoons extra virgin olive oil
2 tablespoons soft white
breadcrumbs
1 tablespoon salted capers,
washed and chopped
2 large anchovy fillets, rinsed, dried
and chopped
1 garlic clove, finely chopped
2 tablespoons chopped fresh
flat-leaf parsley
1 tablespoon pine kernels, chopped
2 tablespoons freshly grated
Parmesan or Pecorino
sea salt and freshly milled
black pepper

Preheat the oven to 375°F/190°C/gas mark 5.

Trim, wash and pat the fish dry. Use one third of the oil to grease an ovenproof dish in which the fish, sandwiched in pairs, will fit snugly side by side. Place two fillets in the dish, skin side down.

Mix together half of the remaining oil with the breadcrumbs, capers, anchovies, garlic, parsley, pine kernels and cheese. Season to taste. Go easy on the salt as the capers, anchovies and cheese are already quite salty. Put this mixture on top of the two fish fillets in the dish, pressing it down quite firmly. Lay the other two fillets on top and press down again. Any remaining filling can be sprinkled over the top .

Drizzle over the rest of the oil and sprinkle lightly with about 2 tablespoons of cold water or dry white wine. Bake in the top part of the oven for about 15 minutes, then leave to rest for about 3 minutes before serving.

Ask your fishmonger to fillet the mackerel so that you can sandwich this delicious filling in between the two fillets and simply bake them in the oven for about 15 minutes. Choose fish of a reasonable size or the dish becomes fiddly to make. This is delicious at any time of the year, but I like it especially in the depths of winter with creamy mashed potato.

barolo chicken
pollo al barolo

SERVES 4

1 oven ready chicken, about
   3.5kg (6 lb)
8 tablespoons olive oil
sea salt and freshly milled
   black pepper
75 g (3 oz) pancetta, finely sliced
1 onion, sliced
1 carrot, sliced
1 stick of celery, sliced
1 bottle youngish Barolo
125 ml (4 fl oz) single cream
white truffle, freshly shaved
   (optional)

Rub the chicken all over inside and out with a little olive oil, season it in the same way and then wrap it carefully in the pancetta.

Heat the remaining oil in a large saucepan and fry the onion, carrot and celery until the vegetables are soft and cooked through. Place the chicken in the pan and seal it all over, then pour in the wine, boil off the alcohol for about 2 minutes, and then lower the heat and leave to simmer slowly, uncovered, for about 1 hour.

Take the chicken out of the sauce and carve it into joints. Wrap in foil and keep warm. Meanwhile, push the liquid and vegetables through a food mill. Return to the saucepan and bring back to boiling point, then remove from the heat and stir in the cream. If you are using truffle, shave in as much as you want or can afford and leave the sauce to stand for a moment. Quickly arrange the chicken joints on a warm serving platter and then pour over the sauce. Serve at once with slices of polenta.

Although the original recipe for this dish uses pheasant, I find that a free range chicken with plenty of flavour also works very well. Use a bottle of fairly young Barolo, or any other intense, full bodied red wine.

tomato and rosemary chicken
pollo al rosmarino e pomodoro

SERVES 4

4 chicken joints, skinned
2 garlic cloves, halved
4 tablespoons olive oil
2 teaspoons fresh chopped
　rosemary leaves or 1 teaspoon
　dried rosemary
400 g (14 oz) canned chopped
　tomatoes
sea salt and freshly milled
　black pepper

Rub the garlic all over the chicken, then chop the garlic finely.

Heat the olive oil in a frying pan, add the chopped garlic and rosemary and fry for about 4 minutes. Add the chicken and brown it thoroughly on all sides.

Pour in the tomatoes, season with salt and pepper and cover. Simmer gently for about 30 minutes, or until the chicken is cooked through. Transfer to a platter and serve immediately with mashed potato and a green vegetable.

pork with leeks
maiale ai porri

SERVES 2

400 g (14 oz) pork loin chops
   or steaks
2 tablespoons plain white flour
2 leeks
2 tablespoons sunflower oil
a small pinch of dried sage
sea salt and freshly milled
   black pepper
4 tablespoons dry white wine
2 teaspoons lemon juice
1 teaspoon lemon zest

Trim the pork and coat it lightly in the flour. Trim and discard the green tops off the leeks and cut them in half. Chop into pieces approximately 2 cm square. Rinse the pieces and dry on kitchen paper.

Heat the oil in a deep sauté pan, add the leeks, sage and plenty of salt and pepper. Fry gently until the leeks are softened and lightly browned.

Raise the heat and add the meat, turning it frequently to brown it all over. Add the wine, lemon juice and zest, stir and lower the heat. Remove half the leeks and set aside. Cover the meat and simmer very gently for about 20 minutes, or until the meat is cooked through and completely tender. Remove the meat and keep it warm.

Puree the leeks in the sauté pan, using a hand-held blender or tipping them into a blender or food processor. Return the meat to the pan with the rest of the leeks and heat through for about 5 minutes, turning frequently. Serve the meat on a warmed platter with the leeks, pouring the leek sauce over the meat. Serve with mashed potato.

A lovely delicate way of flavouring a simple pork dish. If there is any left over, you can eat it cold or mince it and use it as a base for meatballs or meatloaf. At home in Tuscany, pork was never eaten at any other time of the year except for in the winter, so the association of pork and cold weather has always stayed with me.

pork chops with fontina
braciole di maiale con fontina

SERVES 2

2 thick pork chops on the bone
50 g (2 oz) unsalted butter
2 bay leaves
1 sprig of rosemary
sea salt and freshly milled
    black pepper
2 tablespoons brandy
300 g (11 oz) Fontina cheese, sliced

Trim and check the chops to remove bone shards. Melt the butter in an ovenproof casserole and seal the meat all over. Add the bay leaves and rosemary. Lower the heat, season with salt and pepper and continue to cook the meat over a low flame, basting with the brandy and just enough water to keep it all moist.

When the meat is almost cooked through, preheat the oven to 375°F/190°C/gas mark 5. Take the meat out of the casserole and put it on a board. Cut the chops two thirds of the way through and along one side to create a pocket. Insert the slices of cheese into each cut, then close the pocket with a cocktail stick. Return the meat and any meat juices to the casserole and place in the oven for about 15 minutes, until the cheese has melted. Remove the cocktail sticks and serve hot.

Like most meat recipes, this is only worth making if the meat has plenty of flavour and is chewy enough to remind you why you have teeth! Try to always buy really good quality pork which is organically reared. Fontina is far too special a cheese to waste on miserable meat.

mixed bean casserole
fagioli stufati

2 tins cannellini beans, drained
1 tin kidney beans, drained
1 tin chick peas, drained
1 tin haricot beans, drained
1 tin borlotti beans, drained
6 tablespoons olive oil
2 large onions, finely sliced
2 garlic cloves, chopped
a large sprig of rosemary
sea salt and freshly milled
   black pepper
500 ml (16 fl oz) passata

SERVES 4-6

Rinse all the beans in a colander and drain thoroughly.

Heat the olive oil in a large saucepan, and fry the onions and garlic until soft. Add all the beans, the rosemary and seasoning. Pour over the passata, reduce the heat and simmer for 1 hour. Serve hot or cold.

You can use any variety of beans and pulses you like for this dish. Any leftovers can be whizzed in the food processor for a delicious, smooth soup with masses of flavour. I like to serve this on thick slices of crusty Italian bread which I toast, rub with garlic and drizzle with olive oil: it is basically Italian beans on toast!

comforting stew
spezzatino

SERVES 6

1.25 kg (2½ lb) boned pork shoulder
or beef shin
5 tablespoons olive oil
2–3 fresh sage leaves
2–3 sprigs of fresh rosemary
4 tablespoons concentrated tomato
puree, diluted in a teacup of
warm water
400 g (14 oz) canned chopped
tomatoes
stock
500 g (1 lb) potatoes, peeled
and cubed
300 g (10 oz) shelled fresh or
frozen peas
4 large carrots, cut into large cubes
sea salt and freshly milled
black pepper
beef stock for basting

Trim the meat and cut it into cubes. Heat the oil in a casserole with the herbs for a few minutes, then add the meat and seal it all over. Lower the heat and pour in the diluted tomato puree and the tomatoes. Pour in just enough stock to just cover the meat, cover and simmer very gently for about 30–45 minutes, stirring occasionally.

Add the potatoes, peas and carrots. Cover and cook for a further 20–30 minutes, or until the vegetables are cooked. Taste and adjust the seasoning, then transfer to a platter and serve at once with mashed potatoes.

Be sure to give the meat sufficient time to cook so that it becomes really tender, and keep the heat really low so that the liquid around the meat barely moves. This casserole can also be made with game if you prefer.

pandoro filled with cream and zabaglione
pandoro ripieno

SERVES 8

1 large Pandoro (1.5 kg)

double quantity of zabaglione
 (see recipe below)

½ pint whipping cream

6 amaretti biscuits, chopped

125 g (4 oz) plain chocolate
 (preferably Green & Blacks
 organic chocolate), chopped

75 g (3 oz) hazelnuts, shelled and
 toasted, chopped

50 g (2 oz) glacé fruits, chopped

Cut the top off the Pandoro and scoop out some of the interior, leaving a thick shell. Use the discarded Pandoro to make another dessert.

Make the Zabaglione and leave to cool. Whip the cream until soft peaks form and fold in to the zabaglione. Mix all the remaining ingredients and fold gently into the Zabaglione and cream mixture. Spoon this cream into the hollow Pandoro, cover with the top of the cake and chill until required.

zabaglione
zabaglione

SERVES 4

4 egg yolks

4 tablespoons dry Marsala wine

4 tablespoons caster sugar

2 tablespoons cold water

Mix all the ingredients together in a large, heavy bowl or saucepan. Place over another pan of very hot but not boiling water and whisk constantly with an electric hand-held whisk until foaming, pale yellow, thick and shiny. This will take up to 15 minutes.

Pour into stemmed glasses and serve hot, or leave to cool completely and chill before serving or using in another recipe.

spiced pandoro pudding
budino al pandoro

SERVES 6

400 g (14 oz) Pandoro, sliced thinly
    into small rectangles
150 g (5 oz) unsalted butter
150 g (5 oz) raisins, soaked in
    Marsala or brandy for 20 minutes
pinch of ground cloves
pinch of ground cumin
4 egg yolks
75 g (3 oz) caster sugar
500 ml (16 fl oz) double or single
    cream
1 teaspoon vanilla essence
icing sugar for dusting

Preheat oven to gas mark 4/350°F/180°C.

Butter the Pandoro lightly on both sides, then use the remaining butter to grease an ovenproof dish. Arrange one layer of buttered Pandoro slices in the dish, slightly overlapping. Sprinkle with half the raisins, including any remaining liquid. Sprinkle with half the ground spices.

Beat the egg yolks with the caster sugar until pale yellow. Stir in the cream and the vanilla. Mix very thoroughly, then pour half this custard mixture over the Pandoro. Place another layer of Pandoro slices on top, then repeat the layers: raisins, spices and custard mixture. Place the dish in a roasting tin with enough water to come about two thirds up the sides of the dish. Bake until the custard is set and the top lightly golden; this should take about 45 minutes. Just before serving, dust the top of the pudding with icing sugar. Serve warm.

Use any left-over Pandoro as a breakfast treat, spread thinly with butter and thickly with apricot jam. As an alternative to raisins, use dried apricots, chopped finely, then soaked in the same way as the raisins.

orange salad with almonds
insalata di arance con mandorle

SERVES 4

4 large, thin-skinned oranges
4 dessertspoons caster sugar
4 teaspoons orange liqueur or
    orange blossom water
4 dessertspoons sliced almonds,
    toasted

Slice the top off each orange. Place the orange cut side down on a board and use a very sharp, small and flexible knife to slice away the skin. You must cut through the skin and pith to the flesh of the orange, without cutting deep into the actual orange. Cut off the other end of the orange, which you have been holding on to throughout this operation, and then slice the orange into thick discs. Flick out any seeds with the point of the knife. Repeat with all the oranges.

Arrange the slices in a pretty dish. Sprinkle with the sugar, liqueur or orange blossom water and chill. Just before serving, scatter the almonds over the salad.

sweet pastry ribbons
frappe

MAKES ABOUT ½ KG

500 g (1 lb) plain flour
25 g (1 oz) lard
2 egg yolks
1 whole egg
1 tablespoon granulated sugar
pinch of salt
a glass or so white wine
oil for deep-frying
icing sugar for dusting

Mix together the flour, lard, egg yolks and egg, sugar and salt. Gradually add enough wine to make a soft ball of dough, not dissimilar to fresh pasta dough. Let it rest for about 30 minutes.

Roll the dough out finely and cut it into shapes, usually longish wide ribbons.

Heat the oil in a wide, deep pan until a small square of bread dropped into the oil sizzles instantly. Carefully begin to drop a few frappe into the oil, about 6 or 7 in every batch. As soon as they become golden and puffed up and rise to the surface of the oil, scoop them out with a slotted spoon and drain on kitchen paper. Dust with icing sugar and serve warm with chilled Vin Santo.

The chill misery of February is livened up each year by the festivities of Carnevale. To celebrate, all kinds of fried pastries are prepared to eat at parties and while walking around in full costume. The simplest are frappe, which are especially delicious served at the end of a dinner with a glass of dessert wine.

index